Bridging the Gap

In the intricate world of corporate governance, the bridge between the Audit Committee and Internal Audit determines whether an organization sails smoothly toward transparency—or flounders in turbulent waters.

Bridging the Gap: Strengthening the Bond between Audit Committee and Internal Audit is both a compass and a chart for those navigating this essential relationship. Drawing on decades of real-world experience, Denise Cicchella illuminates how communication, trust, and shared purpose transform oversight from formality into foresight.

Through vivid metaphor and grounded guidance, *Bridging the Gap* explores the evolving role of the Audit Committee, the independence of Internal Audit, and the new challenges shaped by technology, regulation, and culture. From handling crises to building confidence, each chapter offers practical strategies for stronger collaboration, ethical leadership, and resilience in the face of change.

Whether you are an Audit Committee member, Chief Audit Executive, board director, or governance professional, this book delivers insight that is both timeless and timely—helping you move from compliance to connection, and from oversight to impact.

Security, Audit and Leadership Series

Series Editor: Dan Swanson, Dan Swanson and Associates, Ltd., Winnipeg, Manitoba, Canada.

The scope and mandate for internal audit continue to evolve each year, as does the complexity of the business environment and speed of the changing risk landscape in which it must operate. The fundamental goal of this exciting series is to produce leading-edge books on critical subjects facing security and audit executives and practitioners. Key topics addressed include Leadership, Cybersecurity, Security Leadership, Privacy, Strategic Risk Management, Auditing IT, Audit Management and Leadership, and Operational Auditing.

Audit Alchemy: Small Teams, BIG Impact – A Guide to Internal Audit Excellence
By *Sandeep Das*

Modern Benford's Law: State of the Art Techniques for Audit and Compliance Professionals
By Daniel J. McCarville

Cumulative Effect: Cyber Security Guide for Directors and CEOs
By Dr Vladas Leonas

Digital Momentum: *Building Real Change-Ready Enterprises*
By Brice Ominski

Redefining Auditing in the Digital Era: *Global Perspectives on Technology, Security, and Leadership*
Edited by Abdelmounim Bouziane

Fire Brigades to Firewalls: *A Public Safety Guide to Cybersecurity*
By John Kuforiji

Bridging the Gap: *Strengthening the Bond between Audit Committee and Internal Audit*
By Denise Cicchella

Bridging the Gap
Strengthening the Bond between Audit Committee and Internal Audit

Denise Cicchella

CRC Press
Taylor & Francis Group
Boca Raton London New York

CRC Press is an imprint of the
Taylor & Francis Group, an **informa** business

Designed cover image: Shutterstock ID: 2467879199

First edition published 2026
by CRC Press
2385 NW Executive Center Drive, Suite 320, Boca Raton FL 33431

and by CRC Press
4 Park Square, Milton Park, Abingdon, Oxon, OX14 4RN

CRC Press is an imprint of Taylor & Francis Group, LLC

Library of Congress Cataloging-in-Publication Data
Names: Cicchella, Denise author
Title: Bridging the gap : strengthening the bond between audit committee and internal audit / Denise Cicchella.
Description: First edition. | Boca Raton : CRC Press, 2026. |
Series: Security, audit and leadership series |
Includes bibliographical references and index. |
Identifiers: LCCN 2026000662 (print) | LCCN 2026000663 (ebook) |
ISBN 9781041077381 hbk | ISBN 9781041078333 pbk | ISBN 9781003642398 ebk
Subjects: LCSH: Audit committees | Auditing, Internal
Classification: LCC HF5667.15 .C53 2026 (print) | LCC HF5667.15 (ebook)
LC record available at https://lccn.loc.gov/2026000662
LC ebook record available at https://lccn.loc.gov/2026000663

ISBN: 9781041077381 (hbk)
ISBN: 9781041078333 (pbk)
ISBN: 9781003642398 (ebk)

DOI: 10.1201/9781003642398

Typeset in Caslon
by Newgen Publishing UK

To every silent sentinel who ever stood watch in the dark, trusting that truth would find its way to daylight. This book is for the guardians of integrity who steady the ship even when no one is watching.

To all the audit executives and audit committee friends that helped me grow in my career and put faith in my wisdom to better their relationships with their audit counterparts.

Contents

Preface

Welcome Aboard the Bridge

There's a certain hush before a ship leaves the harbor. The ropes are loosened, the engines hum beneath your feet, and the crew—some seasoned, some wide-eyed—gather at the rail, looking toward the open water. That's exactly where we stand in the world of audit and governance today: poised on the deck of change, staring at an ocean of possibility, equal parts excitement and uncertainty.

Bridging the Gap is not just a book—it's your boarding pass to that voyage. It's a call to those who navigate the tides of oversight, risk, and accountability to look up from the map and truly see the horizon. The Audit Committee and Internal Audit are two vessels sailing the same sea, each essential, yet too often charting parallel courses. This book is about drawing them together—aligning compass points, setting shared destinations, and hoisting the sails of trust.

When the Audit Committee and Internal Audit operate in harmony, governance doesn't just happen—it glides. The organization moves with balance, agility, and confidence, even when the waves rise high. But when those relationships falter—when communication breaks, when assumptions go unchallenged—the voyage grows perilous. Misunderstanding becomes fog; complacency, the unseen reef.

This guide is both a compass and a conversation. It's filled with stories from the bridge, lessons learned in storm and stillness alike. You'll find practical insights, yes—but also reminders of why this journey matters: integrity, transparency, courage, and human connection. These aren't checkboxes on a compliance form. They're the navigational stars that keep an organization upright when the weather turns.

In these pages, we'll examine what happens when governance meets humanity—when independent oversight becomes interdependent understanding. You'll meet the helmsmen (and women) who steer the committee, the lookouts who scan the horizon, and the deckhands who keep the ropes taut and the lights burning. Together, they form a crew whose success depends not on power, but on partnership.

So welcome aboard. Whether you're a seasoned captain of committees, a first-time internal auditor, or someone who simply believes that integrity should never be left at port, you have a place on this ship. Prepare to question, to laugh, to rethink, and to rediscover what it means to lead from the bridge—steady, strategic, and with the courage to steer toward better waters.

The gangway's up. The engines are turning. Let's sail.

About the Author

Denise Cicchella has spent her career where courage meets clarity, steering organizations toward stronger governance with a blend of insight, empathy, and unwavering integrity. A seasoned auditor who cut her teeth in construction sites, boardrooms, and the unpredictable wilds of real-world oversight, she has become a trusted voice in internal audit, fraud prevention, and organizational leadership.

Her work is rooted in truth telling, bridge building, and empowering teams to speak with purpose. As CEO of Auspicium and a respected trainer, speaker, and author, she helps leaders sharpen their thinking, strengthen their systems, and rise to the responsibilities that shape ethical organizations.

Denise brings a storyteller's heart to a profession often starved for narrative, weaving practical experience with the poetry of possibility. Her writing reflects a life spent walking the line between risk and resilience, always with an eye toward lifting others.

When she is not teaching, writing, or coaching, she can often be found behind a camera, chasing light; in the quiet of nature, listening for new metaphors; or encouraging others to find their own voice and use it with courage.

AI Usage Statement

Artificial intelligence (AI) tools were utilized as part of the writing process for *Bridging the Gap: Strengthening the Bond between Audit Committee and Internal Audit* to enhance clarity, structure, and visual presentation. The primary AI system used was ChatGPT (GPT-5, OpenAI, 2025), which assisted with redrafting, editing, summarizing source material, and refining language consistency across chapters. All content generated or refined through ChatGPT was reviewed, verified, and edited by the author to ensure factual accuracy, contextual appropriateness, and preservation of the author's original intent and professional expertise. In addition, Napkin.ai (2025) was employed to create selected visual elements, including the "Three-Legged Stool" illustration representing acumen, adaptability, and agility. No generative AI outputs were incorporated without human oversight, and no confidential, proprietary, or client-specific information was entered into AI systems at any stage of development. The final manuscript reflects the author's independent analysis, interpretation, and authorship, with AI serving solely as a technical aid to support precision and presentation. AI was used to create the fictional hotel receipt and to show the response from AI in using a tool in this nature.

1

The Helm of Integrity

Understanding Audit Committee's True North

LEADERSHIP IS AN ACTION, NOT A POSITION.

—DONALD MCGANNON

Welcome to *Bridging the Gap: Enhancing the Audit Committee–Auditor Relationship*—a timely exploration into the dynamic dance between audit committees and their closest collaborators: internal and external auditors.

In a world pulsing with complexity, risk, and rapid transformation, the bond between these key players isn't just important—it's mission-critical. When the relationship hums in harmony, oversight becomes sharper, risks are spotted sooner, and organizations stand stronger. But when there's misalignment? Communication falters, trust erodes, and the watchdogs lose their bite.

This isn't just about meetings and memos—it's about building a high-functioning, trust-powered team where transparency, accountability, and candor flow freely. It's about moving from polite formality to purposeful partnership. It's about asking the tough questions, hearing the unvarnished truth, and working together to steward the organization with eyes wide open. It's the open ears around the table filled with mutual respect and understanding.

Go Thee to the Audit Committee

Ah, I remember it vividly—early in my career, huddled in my manager's office with the audit team, when it was suddenly announced that our audit report was heading to the audit committee. I blinked. The *audit*

DOI: 10.1201/9781003642398-1

committee? What did that even *mean*? I glanced at my team leader, and to my surprise, he looked ... sweaty; he looked uneasy. Not the usual confident swagger. Something about that announcement stirred tension in the room.

After the meeting, curiosity got the better of me, so I cornered him. "I see the mention of the audit committee, did not go down well. Who exactly *is* the audit committee?" I asked, half-expecting a list of high-powered names. Instead, he gave a half-smile and said, "They read our reports, reflect on the risks, the findings ... their job is to oversee, to make sure the organization stays on track."

"Okay," I said. "But who *are* they?"

He shrugged. "Honestly? I'm not sure."

It was like he'd said the audit committee, The Wizard of Oz himself—hidden behind a velvet curtain, was unreachable and unknowable. And just like Dorothy and her crew, we were supposed to follow the yellow brick road of governance and accountability ... except our road had "Do Not Enter" signs at every turn. And instead of flying monkeys, there were line managers. They were a riddle wrapped in a suit and tie, an invisible hand steering the ship from the shadows.

But oh, the mystery only made me more intrigued. Who were these masked gatekeepers of oversight? What did they *really* do? It would take me years—years of wandering that winding professional road—before I finally stood face to face with the very committee that once seemed like myth and legend. After that, things fell into place. I no longer feared them, I wanted to work with them, I respected them. I learned who they were and how to talk to them. Pieces of this journey will be shared with you in the pages of the book.

I learned how to partner with *my* audit committee. I will teach you how to do the same.

In this guide, we'll explore the hallmarks of a strong audit committee–auditor alliance:

- Mutual respect, grounded in independence
- Open communication that doesn't wait for the next quarterly meeting
- Shared commitment to integrity, resilience, and long-term value

We'll also tackle the trickier terrain—what to do when tensions rise, how to manage differing expectations, and how to recalibrate when the compass feels off.

Whether you're a seasoned audit chair, a fresh committee recruit, or a forward-thinking auditor, this journey is for you. Let's break down silos, bust myths, and build bridges—because good governance depends on it.

Together, let's redefine the audit relationship: not as a transaction, but as a transformation.

What Is an Audit Committee?

At its heart, an audit committee is a subgroup of a company's board of directors tasked with overseeing the integrity of financial reporting, the effectiveness of internal controls, the risk management framework, and the work of both internal and external auditors. Think of them as the guardians of governance—the truth-tellers who keep financial *fiction* out of the company's story.

But don't let the word "committee" fool you into imagining a sleepy side-show. The audit committee is where the rubber meets the regulatory road. It ensures that what gets reported to investors, regulators, and the public is not only accurate but auditable, explainable, readable, and accountable.

In practical terms, the audit committee:

- Reviews financial statements to make sure they're fair, transparent, and free of "creative accounting."
- Monitors internal controls—those vital checks and balances that prevent fraud and error.
- Engages with external auditors (the independent watchdogs) to ensure objectivity and scope are solid.
- Oversees internal audit to ensure the organization is examining its own health with courage and consistency.
- Keeps an eye on risk—financial, operational, compliance-related, and increasingly, cybersecurity and ESG.
- Serves as a bridge between the board, management, and the auditors—helping align purpose, priorities, and performance.

- Has their own charter—do you know what your audit committee's charter (or mission) is?
- And most importantly, they are the lifeblood of the organization's integrity and the due north on the organization's moral compass.

Audit committees are typically made up of independent non-executive directors, with at least one "financial expert" who can navigate the numbers and sniff out shenanigans. But diversity of thought, background, and experience is also key—today's audit landscape requires more than spreadsheets and sharp pencils.

When the audit committee is strong, the whole organization sleeps better at night. They help build trust with shareholders, enhance transparency, and raise the bar on accountability. They are the sentinels who don't just tick boxes—they ask bold questions, challenge assumptions, and shine a light into the corners. In short, the audit committee is not just a part of good governance. It's the heartbeat of it. Though not normally do for compensation reasons, some audit committees are compensated and a breakdown of compensation by industry can be found in the appendix.

Steering an organization toward truth takes more than compliance; it takes courage at the wheel and conviction in the stars.

2
Crew and Charter
The Framework for Oversight

INTEGRITY IS DOING THE RIGHT THING, EVEN WHEN NO ONE IS WATCHING.

—CS LEWIS

At its core, there are certain factors of the role of audit committee:

> An effective audit committee operates within its purview to ensure financial statements are accurate, concise and readable. It understands the nature of the organization and federal regulation around anti-corruption. It works with corporate management to understand and mitigate fraud in its environment.

Let's break this into some basic tasks.

Assess the Analysis of Important Issues and Judgements Made by Management in or for Financial Reports

One of the audit committee's most vital, yet often underestimated, roles is to scrutinize the judgments and estimates made by management in the financial reporting process. Think of it like checking the stitching beneath the polished surface of a designer gown—it might look flawless on the outside, but what lies beneath determines its integrity.

And this is where the relationship with internal audit becomes a golden thread. Internal audit can help surface areas where management's assumptions may warrant more attention, providing the audit committee with the flashlight needed to illuminate any blind spots.

DOI: 10.1201/9781003642398-2

In a world where stakeholders demand transparency, trust, and truth, the audit committee must step boldly into its role—not just as readers of reports, but as interpreters of intent. They must ask the hard questions, follow the trail of evidence, and when necessary, help steer management back toward the path of prudence.

Behind Every Balance Sheet Is a Story—and It's the Audit Committee's Job to Make Sure It's the *True* One

To fulfill this, the audit committee must remain vigilant and ensure they maintain a clear line of sight over the entire financial reporting process. They should regularly engage with both internal and external auditors, seeking clarity on complex or unusual transactions, and challenging management where necessary. By fostering open dialogue and encouraging a questioning mindset, the audit committee can help prevent groupthink and ensure that financial disclosures genuinely reflect the underlying realities of the organization.

Groupthink is a psychological phenomenon that occurs within a group of people when the desire for harmony or conformity results in irrational or dysfunctional decision-making. In a groupthink situation, members suppress dissenting viewpoints, fail to critically analyze alternatives, and prioritize consensus over the quality of the outcome. This often leads to poor decisions because the group does not adequately consider all options or risks. For an audit committee this can prove to be quite detrimental.

Key characteristics of groupthink include:

- Pressure to conform to the group's views
- Suppression of dissent or alternative opinions
- Illusion of unanimity (everyone appears to agree)
- Overestimation of the group's competence or morality
- Self-censorship by individuals who might otherwise offer objections

Groupthink can be particularly problematic in governance, audit committees, or any decision-making body, as it undermines critical thinking and can result in significant oversights or errors.

Ensure Proper and Appropriate Policies and Procedures for the Prevention and Identification of Fraud

In any organization, fraud prevention is not a one-time effort but a living, breathing framework of vigilance. Audit committees play a critical role in ensuring that proper and appropriate policies and procedures are not only established but actively enforced and regularly refreshed. These mechanisms form the organization's moral immune system—detecting and fighting off deceit before it metastasizes.

Policies should clearly articulate zero tolerance for fraudulent behavior and define responsibilities at every level, from frontline employees to executive management. Procedures should outline robust controls for high-risk areas such as procurement, expense reimbursements, revenue recognition, and third-party relationships, while also promoting ethical conduct and accountability.

However, having a policy on paper is not enough. The audit committee must oversee that these policies are understood, communicated, and embedded into daily operations. Regular fraud risk assessments, whistleblower mechanisms, data analytics for anomaly detection, and continuous training all fortify the organization's fraud defense architecture. By fostering a culture where transparency is championed and ethical courage is rewarded, the audit committee not only guards financial integrity but also reinforces public trust.

In essence, strong policies and procedures are not merely defensive tools—they are the organization's promise to its people and stakeholders that integrity will never be negotiable.

Understand Regulatory Environments and Policies and Procedures around Anti-corruption

Corruption doesn't announce itself with flashing lights and ominous music—it's quieter, sleeker, often dressed in a tailored suit and disguised as "business as usual." It may take the form of a "facilitation payment" in an overseas deal, a lucrative contract awarded to a cousin's company, or a lavish gift exchanged under the guise of "relationship building." And that's exactly why the audit committee must stay sharp, informed, and one step ahead.

In bridging the gap between boardroom strategy and frontline practice, the committee must ask:

- Are we fostering a culture of compliance and ethics, or merely policing infractions after the fact?
- Does management lead by example—or conveniently look the other way when the stakes are high?
- Are we proactive in managing corruption risk—or waiting for a regulator or journalist to point it out?

Because here's the truth: corruption doesn't just hurt profits—it erodes trust, undermines leadership, and shakes investor confidence to the core. The audit committee has a pivotal role in ensuring the organization is on the right side of the law, the right side of history, and—critically—the right side of conscience.

Discuss Quarterly Financial Statements with Management and Auditors

Quarterly financial statements are more than just numbers neatly tucked into tidy columns—they are a real-time pulse check on the organization's financial health, performance, and direction. Each quarter, the audit committee pulls up a seat at the table with both management and auditors, not just to review the data, but to interrogate the story the data tells. This is not about playing financial detective—it's about playing financial *translator*, *truth-teller*, and *tone-checker*. The audit committee must ensure that what's reported to shareholders, regulators, and the public is fair, factual, understandable, and free of spin.

These quarterly dialogues are the committee's opportunity to probe, clarify, and challenge:

- Are revenue figures consistent with business activity?
- Have any accounting policies changed; or have estimates been revised that might impact comparability or perception?
- Are seasonal trends or economic headwinds appropriately disclosed?
- Have there been any one-time adjustments, impairments, or contingencies that need to be explained more transparently?

- Are the statements aligned with internal forecasts, and if not—why?
- Have anomalies been explained with concise, easy to read footnotes or disclosures?

The audit committee shouldn't accept professionally laid out, perfectly collated, glossy summaries at face value. They should *ask why*, *dig deeper*, and understand the "so what" behind each financial decision and disclosure. Results perfectly bonded, in color and neat binds, may show that the statements are of high quality, but audit committee must look behind the pretty presentation and question the guts beneath.

When management presents the quarterly numbers, the committee must also seek assurance from the external and internal auditors. These discussions should explore:

- Any areas where auditors disagreed with management—or had to negotiate interpretations.
- Any areas where management refused to cooperate and audits had to be scaled back on scope.
- Materiality thresholds: What's in, what's out, and why?
- Risk indicators or anomalies the auditors flagged during their procedures.
- Any concerns about internal controls, fraud risk, or aggressive or creative accounting treatments.
- Trends that don't make sense or do not gel with reports on recent events and activities.

By hearing both perspectives—the preparers *and* the checkers—the audit committee ensures the narrative is complete and credible. Quarterly financial reviews are one of the most powerful tools for bridging the gap between governance and execution. They allow the audit committee to:

- Spot trends early—before they become headlines.
- Identify subtle shifts in business strategy or risk posture.
- Encourage consistency and discipline in financial communication.

And most importantly, these meetings help maintain a tone of transparency and accountability from the top. The best audit committees don't wait for the year-end audit to uncover red flags. They use the quarterly rhythm to create a culture of ongoing oversight, turning financial review into a dialogue, not a download. After all, when you talk through the numbers regularly, openly, and with the right people at the table, you're not just reviewing the past, you're steering the future.

Ensure Successful Merger and Acquisition (M&A) Transactions, if One Should Occur

Ready to shake hands on a new deal? Mergers and acquisitions—those grand, strategic chess moves that promise growth, market share, innovation … and occasionally, chaos. When organizations pursue these high-stakes deals, the room fills with excitement, ambition, and a touch of corporate adrenaline. But beneath the headlines and handshakes lies a minefield of financial, operational, legal, and reputational risk. Vulnerabilities become focused and fraud and error must be carefully investigated. Workers unsure of their future may not be as diligent and careful as they should be.

Enter the audit committee: not to lead the charge, but to fortify the foundation, ensuring that if the organization does take this leap, it lands with both feet and eyes wide open.

While M&A is typically seen as the domain of executives and corporate strategists, the audit committee plays a critical supporting role, particularly in due diligence, risk management, and post-transaction integration oversight. Their job isn't to decide *if* a deal should happen, but to make sure that if it does, it's executed with discipline, clarity, honesty, and strong internal controls.

Due Diligence Assurance

Before any ink hits the contract, the audit committee must ensure that robust due diligence has been performed. Are the target company's financials accurate and verifiable? What are the hidden liabilities, pending lawsuits, or off-balance sheet exposures? Are there any ticking time bombs in their tax structures or compliance history? Audit committee should also question if there are any nasty ink blots in the past or future about the company. For example, pending lawsuits, even if occurring before the M&A date, leave a trace of guilt by association.

Internal Control Compatibility

Will the merged entity's systems and processes align with the acquiring organization's control environment? Are there gaps that might introduce fraud risk or compliance failure? Audit committees must ask whether both cultures are *ready* to integrate, especially when it comes to ethics, governance, and financial reporting.

It's essential to examine whether the target company's internal controls align with your own organization's standards. Are their processes for financial reporting, compliance, and risk management robust and compatible, or will gaps and inconsistencies pose a threat during integration? The audit committee should press for a thorough assessment of both entities' control environments, highlighting any areas requiring remediation or harmonization before the deal proceeds. This careful scrutiny can significantly reduce the risk of post-merger surprises or control weaknesses emerging down the line. All that being said, the companies may not be open and honest to admit faults, especially if this can compromise the overall transaction.

Valuation Justification

Is the price being paid based on real, tangible value—or on future dreams and overzealous projections? Audit committees should question the assumptions underpinning the valuation:

- revenue forecasts,
- cost synergies,
- goodwill estimates, and
- integration costs.

Regulatory and Legal Risk

Has the legal team flagged any antitrust, anti-corruption, or compliance issues that could derail or delay the deal? In cross-border transactions, has local regulation been fully considered? Have all regulatory approvals been secured?

Post-transaction Audit Oversight

The job doesn't end with the closing bell. Post-merger, the audit committee should monitor the integration of accounting systems, the consistency of internal controls, and the financial impact of the transaction. Are there early warning signs of deal fatigue, cultural misalignment, or performance shortfalls?

When M&A is on the horizon, the audit committee becomes a vital bridge between strategic ambition and financial discipline. They ensure that the company doesn't fall so in love with the idea of the deal that it forgets to tie its own shoelaces. Their voice is often the calm in the whirlwind, asking the hard questions when everyone else is racing toward the "go-live" date.

And their partnership with internal audit becomes even more critical: internal audit can be tasked with conducting pre- and post-acquisition reviews, spotlighting emerging risks, and verifying whether integration milestones are being met.

Here's the bottom line: a successful acquisition isn't measured by headlines—it's measured by sustained value, (perceived) honesty, adherence to promises and contractual rights/responsibilities, cultural alignment, and control stability. And that's where the audit committee earns its stripes—not in the boardroom celebration, but in the careful, thoughtful work that ensures the company *grows wisely*, not just *quickly*.

Appoint and Compensate External Auditor

In the great theater of corporate governance, the external auditor plays the role of truth-teller—a neutral voice in a room full of competing interests. But who casts that leading actor in the first place? Who ensures they're not only competent and credible, but also independent, fair, and appropriately compensated?

That sacred responsibility rests with the audit committee.

Appointing and compensating the external auditor isn't a mere formality—it's a cornerstone of organizational integrity and stakeholder trust. The audit committee must approach this task with a discerning eye, a strong backbone, and a commitment to quality over convenience.

Selecting the Right Partner

When it's time to appoint—or reappoint—an auditor, the committee must go beyond brand names and fees. They should ask:

- Does the firm have the relevant industry expertise and bench strength to handle our complexity?
- Who will lead the engagement? What's their track record? Are they appropriately licensed? Do they understand the industry?
- Is the proposed audit approach risk-based, forward-looking, and tailored to our business?
- Does the auditor demonstrate independence—not just technically, but in tone, conduct, and courage?
- Have we worked with them before? For how long? What were the results?
- Have they been flagged with any current or pending litigation or legislation occurrences?
- Are they someone we can trust working with?
- If wrongdoing should occur with this company, how would we, as an organization, be seen by the *real world*?

Whether it's a Big Four giant or a regional powerhouse, the auditor must be able to challenge management without fear, dig into the dark corners, and bring uncomfortable truths to light—professionally, respectfully, and fearlessly.

Compensating with Care

Audit fees are a delicate dance. Too low, and you risk a rushed audit or inexperienced staff. Too high, and stakeholders will question efficiency. The audit committee must ensure fees are commensurate with scope, quality, and risk, not just based on what was paid last year. They should ensure that bills coming in reflect services received.

They should:

- Benchmark fees against similar companies or industries.
- Understand what's included—and what's considered "out of scope."
- Consider how changes in operations (e.g., acquisitions, system upgrades, geographic expansion) affect audit effort and cost.

Maintaining Independence

This is where the bridge between oversight and ethics becomes vital.

The audit committee must:

- Review non-audit services provided by the auditor to avoid threats to independence.
- Approve all additional services in advance and ensure they don't impair objectivity.
- Rotate lead partners periodically and consider audit firm rotation if needed to refresh perspective.

After a while, especially if the same staff is being used over and over, an air of comfort between auditor and auditee is likely to form. This may be on the luscious greens of the back nine or within the polished mahogany of the boardroom. However, auditors must maintain *professional skepticism.* This is a mindset to trust the evidence they are given but also to question and validate its authenticity. Familiarity and relationships with the auditor may cloud this professional skepticism.

In essence, they guard the line between collaboration and coziness—ensuring the auditor is close enough to understand the business, but far enough to remain impartial.

Appointing and compensating the external auditor isn't a behind-the-scenes human resources task—it's a strategic governance function that touches on risk, reputation, and reporting.

This balancing act requires ongoing vigilance. The audit committee should periodically assess the quality of the auditor–client relationship, ensuring that open communication does not cross into undue familiarity. Regular training and updates on emerging threats to independence, including evolving regulatory requirements and professional standards, are essential to reinforce the auditor's objectivity and keep ethical considerations at the forefront of the engagement.

By taking a thoughtful, transparent, and principled approach, the audit committee sends a powerful message: we value truth over comfort, independence over convenience, and quality over routine.

When the numbers matter most—when things go wrong, or when shareholders demand answers—it's the external auditor's voice that echoes the loudest. And the audit committee? They're the ones who decided who got the microphone in the first place.

Oversee Internal Audit

Internal audit is the organization's watchtower—scanning for risk, exposing blind spots, and illuminating inefficiencies before they erode value. But who watches the watchtower? That's where the audit committee comes in—not as a supervisor in the traditional sense, but as an independent, strategic ally who ensures that internal audit is empowered, equipped, and positioned to deliver its highest value.

> And here's the key: this oversight responsibility holds firm regardless of where internal audit sits in the organizational hierarchy.

Whether the Chief Audit Executive (CAE) reports directly to the CEO, the CFO, or even the board chair, the audit committee ideally holds the governance compass—ensuring independence, objectivity, and access.

What Does Oversight Look Like?

Independence and Objectivity

The audit committee must ensure that internal audit has true operational independence—not just on paper. That means:

- No interference with audit plans, scope, or findings.
- The CAE has direct and unrestricted access to the audit committee.
- The committee meets with the CAE in executive session (without management)/regularly to create a safe space for open dialogue.

Approve the Internal Audit Charter and Plan

Oversight means engagement, not micromanagement. The committee should:

- Review and approve the internal audit charter to confirm its purpose, authority, and responsibilities.
- Discuss and approve the risk-based audit plan, ensuring it aligns with organizational priorities and emerging risks.

- Ask: Are we covering the right areas? Are we revisiting the same low-risk functions, or are we addressing what really keeps us up at night?
- Listen: Accept that the CAE has made decisions for certain reasons. Not every decision is yes or no, many decisions have layers of grey so CAE should have a chance to discuss reasons certain decisions were made.
- The committee should have a relationship of professional skepticism and should not feel like any questions they have are ignored or skipped or worse yet, not asked, as they were afraid to ask for clarification.
- Ensure that internal audit has the resources it needs and spearhead any efforts to get more.

Resource Support

A brilliant plan is only as good as the team behind it. The committee ensures that internal audit has:

- The budget, tools, and talent required to do the job right.
- Access to specialists in areas like cybersecurity, data analytics, or Environmental, Social, and Governance (ESG) when needed.
- Opportunities for ongoing professional development—because today's risks evolve quickly, and so must the auditors.

Monitor Quality and Performance

Oversight also means accountability. The committee should:

- Review internal audit's performance metrics, completion rates, and impact.
- Ensure periodic external quality assessments are conducted per IIA standards.
- Solicit feedback from auditees and senior leadership to gauge audit's effectiveness and influence.
- Ensure that the audit team has the team and budget to take training necessary to maintain their certifications and grow in their roles.

- Make sure the audit team has private access to the audit committee where no others can overhear or observe what is being said.
- Ask any questions for clarification of completeness that may be missing from reports.

Encourage Courage

One of the most powerful things an audit committee can do is create a culture where internal audit feels safe to speak up—even when the message is uncomfortable. Auditors should never feel pressured to soften a finding or avoid a politically charged issue. This is why the need for private access to the committee is crucial. Audit may find sensitive information about management or executives and they need to feel safe to discuss it. The committee needs to be the voice of internal audit, even when internal audit can speak for themselves.

The committee can ask:

- Are internal audit's recommendations being taken seriously by management?
- Are issues being closed out on time—or endlessly deferred?
- Are there trends in findings that hint at systemic weaknesses?
- Is the audit committee receiving resistance to items asked for, management action plans or access to certain records/projects/departments?
- Are there any issues or questions where audit "clams up" or seems reluctant to discuss issues?

> This is the heartbeat of the audit committee's relationship with internal audit: support without control, access without interference, and partnership without compromise.

The goal is to champion an internal audit function that is not just a compliance box-checker, but a trusted advisor—forward-thinking, solution-oriented, and deeply aligned with the organization's mission.

Because no matter where internal audit reports within the hierarchy, the audit committee holds the flashlight—ensuring internal audit has both the freedom and the focus to shine that light where it matters most.

Ensure Compliance with Rules and Regulations

Let's be honest, the term "compliance" doesn't always make hearts race. But make no mistake: when it's ignored, it can stop a company in its tracks! From regulatory fines to reputational ruin, the cost of non-compliance is steep and unforgiving. That's why the audit committee must serve as both sentinel and steward, ensuring the organization not only knows the rules of the game but *actually* plays by them.

But it goes deeper than legal boxes and policy binders. This is about creating a culture where ethics aren't optional, and where doing the right thing isn't just the slogan on the office wall—it's the expectation, from the boardroom to the break room.

The Two Pillars: Compliance and Conduct

Compliance with Laws and Regulations

The audit committee must ensure that management has built strong structures to monitor and adapt to a constantly evolving regulatory landscape. This includes

- Financial regulations (e.g., Sarbanes Oxley (SOX), International Financial Reporting Standards (IFRS), Generally Accepted Accounting Principles (GAAP) standards, tax codes)
- Industry-specific laws (e.g., Health Insurance Portability and Accounting Standards (HIPAA) for healthcare, General Data Protection Regulation (GDPR) for data privacy, ESG disclosure mandates)
- Global compliance risks for multinational organizations (e.g., sanctions, export controls, anti-money laundering)

The committee should ask:

- Is there a compliance function with the expertise, independence, and authority to act?

- How is management kept abreast of changes to rules and regulations that affect them?
- Are policies reviewed regularly to keep pace with new rules?
- How does the organization monitor changes in law—and how quickly does it respond?
- Are violations investigated swiftly and transparently, and are lessons learned embedded into future practices?
- When non-compliance is noted, has a cause–effect analysis been done? Was the non-compliance malicious or due to lack of proper training or another reason?

Code of Conduct and Ethical Standards

The Code of Conduct is more than just an onboarding document—it's the organization's ethical north star. The audit committee ensures it's not only well-written but well-lived. That means:

- Clear expectations for behavior across all levels—executives, employees, contractors, and third parties.
- Specific guidance on issues like bribery, harassment, discrimination, conflicts of interest, and misuse of company assets.

They ensure whistleblower channels that are safe, accessible, and acted upon—not ignored or buried.

The committee should also review:

- Training programs: Are employees regularly reminded of their ethical obligations?
- Tone at the top: Do leaders model the conduct they expect from others?
- Disciplinary consistency: Is misconduct handled with fairness, not favoritism?

This is where the audit committee moves from governance into guardianship—not of rules alone, but of the organization's reputation, resilience, and right to operate.

> Compliance without integrity is fragile. And integrity without accountability is hollow.

The committee ensures that the two walk hand in hand, supported by strong policies, an empowered compliance function, and a boardroom that backs words with action.

At the end of the day, ethics is the foundation of trust, and trust is the currency of longevity. In a world where one scandal can unravel decades of goodwill, the audit committee must champion not just the letter of the law—but the spirit of it.

Because companies don't rise and fall on profits alone. They rise and fall on principles.

Trust is built like architecture—brick by principle, beam by purpose, bound together by transparency.

3

The Golden Thread

Weaving Audit Committee into the Sail of Governance

TRUST ARRIVES ON FOOT BUT LEAVES ON HORSEBACK.

—DUTCH PROVERB

Not every company needs nor wants an audit committee, but for publicly traded companies, it's a game-changer! Regulatory bodies like the Securities and Exchange Commission (SEC) mandate it to ensure independent oversight of financial reporting, internal controls, and audit functions. For private companies, having an audit committee can still be a game-changer, enhancing governance, improving financial reporting accuracy, and adding an extra layer of oversight and accountability.

So why have an Audit Committee—the quiet powerhouse of corporate governance?

Because in a world spinning with risk, regulation, and reputational landmines, the Audit Committee is the compass, the guardrail, and the conscience of the boardroom, all rolled into one.

At its heart, having an Audit Committee signals to the world that a company is serious about stewardship. It's a public pledge to play fair, account accurately, and face scrutiny with grace. This isn't just about ticking a compliance box; it's about weaving trust into the corporate fabric.

Companies opt for Audit Committees because they bring focus. When the full board has a banquet of responsibilities, from strategy to succession planning—it helps to have a dedicated table where the financials, the risks, the controls, and the audit conversations can be

DOI: 10.1201/9781003642398-3

properly chewed over. The Audit Committee is that table. They slice through the noise, ask the awkward questions (hopefully), and ensure that what's whispered in the margins gets brought into the spotlight.

There's also the issue of independence. A well-composed Audit Committee brings together directors who are not only financially literate but emotionally detached from the day-to-day grind of the company. That detachment is power. It means they can listen without bias, review without flattery, and challenge without fear. But are they given the tools they need? We will find out as we explore the delicate balance of Audit Committee–Auditor relationships.

And now, as the world tilts ever more toward sustainability, ethics, and accountability, the Audit Committee is increasingly stepping into the Environmental, Social, and Governance (ESG) arena. ESG issues are no longer soft topics—they're hard metrics, tracked, rated, and scrutinized by investors, regulators, and society at large. The Audit Committee's role is evolving to ensure that ESG reporting has the same backbone as financial reporting—rooted in evidence, anchored in assurance, and free from rhetoric and exaggerated efforts that are not being met.

> When ESG meets audit, it becomes more than a story—it becomes a system of record.

To Be or Not to Be—Chained with an Audit Committee

For publicly listed companies, forming an Audit Committee isn't just wise—it's often mandatory, a requirement set by regulators and stock exchanges to protect shareholders and uphold market integrity. But even with private companies, non-profits, or public sector entities, the rationale holds. Whether you're a Fortune 500 giant or a quietly ambitious enterprise, an Audit Committee can be the difference between surface-level oversight and deep, resilient governance.

So, why do companies form an Audit Committee? Because it's a signal of maturity. It's a structure that brings discipline. It's a forum for truth-telling. And most importantly, it's an essential link in the chain of trust between management, the board, the auditors, and the stakeholders watching from the wings.

Adapting to Evolving Responsibilities

The role of audit committees will continue to evolve as new regulations and standards are introduced. Audit committees will need to adapt their practices and focus areas to meet these changing demands, ensuring effective oversight in a rapidly changing business environment.

The role of audit committees is not carved in stone—it's etched in sand, constantly reshaped by the tides of regulation, risk, and stakeholder expectation. As new standards emerge and frameworks evolve—be it ESG disclosures under the EU's Corporate Sustainability Reporting Directive, AI governance, cyber risk accountability, or updated internal control models—audit committees must remain agile, not anchored.

This means shedding the "checklist mentality" and embracing a dynamic, forward-looking approach to oversight. Yesterday's compliance comfort zones won't hold up against tomorrow's demands for transparency, ethics, and strategic risk navigation.

Adaptation will involve more than just staying informed—it will require recalibrating agendas, upskilling committee members, and collaborating more closely with management, internal audit, and external advisors. Audit committees will need to sharpen their focus on emerging risk landscapes, such as climate-related financial impacts, algorithmic bias, and geopolitical volatility, while ensuring that the fundamentals—financial integrity, internal controls, and ethical culture—remain robust.

In essence, the audit committee must evolve from being a reactive reviewer to a strategic sentry—one that sees around corners, connects the dots, and helps steer the organization through regulatory fog with clarity and confidence.

In our current world of constant risk changes, new threats, new regulations, audit committees muse be able to pivot as well as Lebron James.

Continuous Improvement and Learning

Audit committees will need to prioritize continuous improvement and learning to stay ahead of emerging trends and challenges. This includes staying informed about best practices, participating in ongoing training and development, and fostering a culture of continuous improvement within the organization. In a world where risk never sleeps and regulations evolve in real time, standing still is not an option.

Audit committees must lead with a mindset of continuous improvement and lifelong learning—not just as a best practice, but as a strategic imperative.

This means more than the occasional refresher course. It calls for a proactive commitment to staying ahead of the curve—monitoring emerging risks, benchmarking against leading practices, and engaging with evolving standards in areas like ESG, cybersecurity, AI ethics, and financial reporting.

The most effective audit committees are not just composed of experienced professionals; they're composed of curious professionals—those who ask better questions, seek better insights, and never assume yesterday's answers are sufficient for today's complexities. It also means investing in training and development, not only for the committee itself but for the broader governance ecosystem.

When the board learns, the business benefits.

Encouraging continuous upskilling—through workshops, webinars, roundtables, or scenario-based simulations—ensures that committee members bring fresh, relevant thinking to every meeting.

Finally, audit committees must model the very culture they seek to instill across the organization: one that embraces improvement, encourages reflection, and sees learning as a strength, not a sign of deficiency. In doing so, they set the tone from the top—demonstrating that resilience and relevance are built not on what you know today, but on your ability to learn, adapt, and lead tomorrow.

So, while not every company *has* to have an Audit Committee, those that do are playing the long game. It's a move that says, "We're serious about doing things right." It's not just about box-ticking or boardroom formalities—it's about building trust, keeping the financial house in order, and making sure the future doesn't arrive with any nasty surprises. In the world of good governance, an Audit Committee isn't just best practice—it's best instinct.

In a world that never stops shifting—whether it's tech disruptions, geopolitical tremors, or the ever-changing tide of stakeholder expectations—the Audit Committee becomes a company's stabilizing force. It's the crew in the crow's nest, scanning the horizon for risk and opportunity, ready to help steer when the winds change.

With their firm grip on financials, controls, and emerging risks, the Audit Committee doesn't just make pivoting possible—it makes it safer. They bring perspective when pressure mounts, clarity when confusion creeps in, and accountability when action is needed. In uncertain times, they're not the ones yelling "brace for impact"—they're the ones calmly helping the ship change course before the storm ever hits.

In this new world, this means that audit committee commitments may require a larger commitment of time than it used to. In this new world of ever-evolving risks, complex regulations, and soaring stakeholder expectations, the role of the audit committee is no longer a side gig—it's a full-on, all-hands-on-deck mission. What once might have been satisfied with quarterly meetings and surface-level reviews now demands a deeper dive, sharper focus, and more frequent engagement.

Audit committee members will find themselves called upon to spend significantly more time—not just in meetings, but preparing, learning, and collaborating across functions. They'll need to immerse themselves in emerging issues like ESG disclosures, cyber resilience, AI ethics, and global supply chain risks. This isn't just about ticking boxes anymore; it's about truly understanding the shifting landscape and guiding the organization through uncharted waters. It is also no longer sufficient to look ahead to the future; audit committees need to look forward, backward and side to side to keep up a 360-degree focus.

The commitment is no longer just about attendance; it's about active stewardship, thoughtful challenge, and strategic foresight. Time once dedicated to routine financial oversight must now be shared with broader governance conversations, risk appetite recalibrations, and sustainability commitments.

Simply put, audit committee members must be ready to invest more time and energy than ever before—because the stakes have never been higher and the need for vigilance never greater. A great teacher of internal audit said a few years ago, that if you wait to do an annual risk assessment, the bus has left without you. It has never been truer than now. Annual risk assessments are no longer valuable as businesses pivot and pivot and pivot at every turn.

The Power of Audit Committees in Corporate Governance

Audit committees are the unsung heroes of corporate governance. They ensure the integrity and transparency of financial reporting, which is fundamental to maintaining stakeholder confidence. Here's why they are so essential:

- Oversight of Financial Reporting: Audit committees oversee the financial reporting process, ensuring accuracy and reliability. This prevents errors and fraud, protecting shareholders and stakeholders. It enables full transparency for current investors and helps attract new ones, becoming the Miracle-Gro that fuels corporate valuation and long-term growth.
- Risk Management: By working closely with internal and external auditors, audit committees help identify and manage risks within the organization, ensuring all significant risks are effectively identified and managed. This collaboration fosters a robust risk culture where emerging threats are flagged early, and mitigation strategies are thoughtfully developed. Through ongoing dialogue and review, audit committees gain critical insights that enable them to challenge assumptions, support proactive decision-making, and safeguard the organization's long-term resilience.
- Compliance with Laws and Regulations: Audit committees ensure the organization complies with applicable laws and regulations, overseeing the entire compliance framework. They act as vigilant guardians, monitoring the effectiveness of policies, controls, and procedures designed to prevent violations and ethical lapses. By fostering a culture of accountability and transparency, audit committees help the organization navigate complex regulatory landscapes, reducing legal risks and protecting its reputation in an ever-changing environment.
- Fraud Prevention and Detection: Audit committees ensure the organization complies with applicable laws and regulations, overseeing the entire compliance framework. In today's increasingly complex environment, their role extends beyond traditional compliance to include a proactive stance on forensic auditing—the deep dive investigations that uncover fraud,

misconduct, and financial irregularities. With rising risks of cybercrime, data breaches, and sophisticated financial manipulation, audit committees must ensure internal audit functions are equipped not only to detect but to anticipate and respond to these threats. This means supporting forensic audit capabilities that combine technology, data analytics, and investigative expertise to protect the organization's integrity. By integrating forensic auditing into their oversight, audit committees strengthen the organization's defense against fraud and contribute to a culture of ethical vigilance and transparency.

- Operational Efficiency: Audit committees ensure that recommendations from both internal and external audits are implemented effectively, leading to more efficient operations. By actively tracking and following up on these recommendations, they help close gaps in controls and processes that could otherwise expose the organization to risk or inefficiency. This diligent oversight fosters a culture of continuous improvement, where lessons learned translate into stronger governance and enhanced organizational performance.
- Stakeholder Confidence: Effective audit committees enhance stakeholder confidence, assuring them that the organization is managed effectively, and its financial statements are reliable. Their rigorous oversight assures investors, regulators, and other stakeholders that the company's financial statements are accurate, complete, and free from material misstatements. Beyond numbers, they signal that the organization is managed with integrity and foresight, inspiring trust that risks are identified and managed, and that the business is positioned for sustainable success in a complex and ever-changing environment.

When it comes to sharing audit committee findings beyond the boardroom, discretion is both shield and sail. The committee's challenge is to communicate with clarity while protecting the integrity of confidential information, especially when the subject involves sensitive financial results, compliance lapses, or control weaknesses. External communication should always be purpose-driven—anchored in transparency, not exposure. A well-defined communication protocol, developed jointly with management and legal counsel, helps ensure that disclosures serve the organization's mission and comply with all regulatory and ethical boundaries. This means choosing what to share, when to share it, and with whom, in a way that strengthens stakeholder trust rather than feeding speculation.

True transparency is not the same as full disclosure. The audit committee must learn to tell the truth without telling every detail. Summarizing themes, trends, or assurance outcomes in plain language—while omitting proprietary or identifying information—allows the committee to demonstrate oversight without breaching confidence. Annual reports, shareholder meetings, or corporate sustainability statements provide opportunities to communicate at this strategic altitude: discussing how the committee approaches risk, ethics, and control, rather than recounting every finding.

Finally, tone matters as much as content. Communication should convey accountability, not alarm. When the committee speaks externally, it speaks on behalf of the organization's conscience, not its secrets. Clear, factual language supported by data-driven context invites confidence, while measured transparency signals maturity in governance. In short, when audit committees master the art of communicating with integrity and restraint, they prove that confidentiality and accountability can coexist on the same bridge.

> Trust is a fragile thread—easily frayed, yet essential to the fabric of any organization's success.

For audit committees, preserving trust is both a solemn duty and a strategic imperative. They stand as the custodians of integrity, ensuring that financial disclosures are truthful, risks are transparently managed, and ethical standards are unwaveringly upheld.

Every decision, every oversight action, sends a signal to investors, employees, and the wider market that the organization values honesty and accountability. In an era where skepticism runs high and reputations can be shattered overnight, the audit committee's role in safeguarding trust is not just about compliance—it's about cultivating confidence that becomes the foundation for enduring relationships and long-term value.

Despite their importance, Audit Committees often face several challenges that can impact their effectiveness and ability to fulfill their responsibilities. Here are some common challenges:

1. Conflicts and disagreements
2. Handling regulatory changes and external pressures
3. Limited resources
4. Conflicting stakeholder interests
5. Evolving compliance standards
6. Maintaining audit integrity and effectiveness

We discuss these in more detail later on.

The Vital Role of the PCAOB

The Public Company Accounting Board (PCAOB) emphasizes the vital role of audit committees in promoting high-quality auditing. An engaged and informed audit committee is a force multiplier in promoting audit quality for the benefit of investors. The PCAOB interacts directly with audit committee chairs, providing timely and relevant information on auditor independence, communications, inspections reports, audit quality, and critical audit matters.

PCAOB is a non-profit corporation that was established by Congress, via the Sarbanes Oxley Act of 2002, to oversee the audits of public companies and SEC-registered brokers and dealers. The PCAOB's mission is to protect investors and further the public interest in the preparation of informative, accurate, and independent audit reports.

The PCAOB has four primary duties:

1. Register public accounting firms that prepare audit reports for issuers, and SEC-registered brokers and dealers.
2. Establish or adopt auditing and related attestation, quality control, ethics, and independence standards.
3. Inspect registered public accounting firms' audits and quality control systems.
4. Investigate and discipline registered public accounting firms and their associated persons for violations of specified laws, rules, or professional standards.

In support of its mission, the PCAOB also conducts economic research and risk analysis, engages with stakeholders and other domestic and international regulators, and manages a talented workforce and the technology and resources needed to perform its duties.

When it comes to audit committees, the PCAOB may not prescribe a rigid checklist of qualifications, but it certainly paints a clear picture of what *responsible oversight* looks like. It doesn't spell out who should be on the committee—that's largely left to the SEC and stock exchange requirements—but it does set strong expectations for how audit committees should operate, particularly in their stewardship of the external audit process.

The PCAOB's core focus is on *engagement*. Not the passive, nodding-head variety, but full-bodied, sleeves-rolled-up involvement in the audit process. Under Auditing Standard 1301, auditors are required to communicate key matters to the audit committee—things like the overall audit strategy and timing, significant risks (especially fraud-related ones), critical accounting estimates, and any major unusual transactions. But it's not enough to receive these updates. The audit committee must actively listen, ask insightful questions, and engage in honest, sometimes tough, two-way dialogue with the auditor. In short, the committee isn't a quiet observer—it must be the protagonist in the story of financial accountability.

Another high-priority area is independence. The PCAOB emphasizes that the audit committee must be the gatekeeper of the auditor's independence. That means reviewing all services—both audit and non-audit—before they begin, watching for conflicts of interest, and maintaining a healthy arm's-length relationship. The committee must ensure that the referee isn't secretly playing for the team it's meant to oversee.

In recent years, PCAOB inspection reports and public statements have spotlighted what they call the "tone at the top." It's a subtle but significant concept. The PCAOB wants to see audit committees fostering a culture of transparency and challenge—not one of complacency. That means asking the right questions, expecting high-quality answers, and reinforcing a standard of rigor in financial reporting and control. Audit quality isn't just the auditor's responsibility—it's a team sport, and the audit committee is the captain.

While the PCAOB doesn't issue rules on committee composition, its guidance resonates in harmony with requirements from the SEC and stock exchanges, such as having independent members, at least one financial expert, and overall financial literacy. These foundational elements help create a committee capable of executing the PCAOB's vision: a curious, courageous, and fully accountable team.

In more recent years, the PCAOB's leadership has grown increasingly vocal about emerging risks. From the rise of cybersecurity threats and ESG disclosures to the influence of artificial intelligence in financial systems, the PCAOB expects audit committees to remain proactive. That means staying informed, adapting their oversight, and continuing to challenge auditors to rise to the evolving complexity of today's business environment.

So, while the PCAOB doesn't hand down a golden list of qualifications or a formal mandate, it does issue a very clear call to action. Audit committees are expected to move beyond ceremonial governance into the realm of gritty, meaningful oversight—challenging assumptions, defending integrity, and being vigilant stewards of audit quality.

Audit Committee and the SEC

According to the SEC, every audit committee must be made up entirely of independent directors. That means no ties—financial, familial, or professional—that could compromise objectivity. Independence is defined quite strictly: audit committee members must not accept any consulting, advisory, or other compensatory fees from the company or its subsidiaries, nor be affiliated persons of the company.

Moreover, each audit committee must include at least one "financial expert." This doesn't necessarily mean a Certified Public Accountant (CPA) or Chief Financial Officer (CFO), but the individual must have:

- An understanding of generally accepted accounting principles (GAAP)
- Experience preparing, auditing, analyzing, or evaluating financial statements
- An understanding of internal controls and procedures for financial reporting

The financial expert must be disclosed in public filings. If a company doesn't have one, it must explain why. For non-U.S. companies listed in the United States, there are limited exceptions—but even then, the SEC requires functional equivalents of audit committees that comply with most of the same rules. No one gets a total pass.

Under Rule 10A-3 of the Exchange Act, the SEC outlines non-negotiable duties for audit committees. These include:

- Appointing, compensating, and overseeing the work of the external auditor. The audit committee, not management, is the auditor's boss.
- Pre-approving all audit and permitted non-audit services. No rubber-stamping, no surprises.
- Establishing procedures for handling complaints related to accounting, internal controls, and auditing matters. This includes anonymous whistleblower submissions—an early warning system for financial mischief.
- Ensuring auditor independence. The audit committee must monitor ongoing independence, not just check a box at appointment time.

The SEC's minimum requirements for audit committees are *deliberate, detailed, and decisive*. They don't just want a committee—they want an independent, qualified, and empowered committee. The kind that doesn't merely observe, but acts. The kind that doesn't fold under pressure, but questions, probes, and persists.

Uniting Internal Audit, Audit Committee, and External Audit

Earlier, we discussed the evolving role of the audit committee and the many directions they must extend to meet new responsibilities. Yet, they don't face this challenge alone—they serve as the commander-in-chief, leading multiple battalions: Internal Audit and External Audit. Understanding why internal audit, external audit, and the audit committee need to be unified in their efforts is crucial for several reasons.

Enhanced Risk Management

A unified team provides a comprehensive view of the organization's risk landscape, ensuring all significant risks are identified and managed effectively. The audit committee cannot be everywhere, so it must rely on multiple eyes to help them focus the full picture.

Improved Financial Reporting and Stakeholder Confidence

Unified efforts ensure financial statements are accurate and reliable. Allowing the crucial transparency the investors want, deliver this to them and the entire relationship can prosper. A unified team enhances stakeholder confidence, assuring them that the organization is managed effectively, and its financial statements are reliable.

Compliance and Governance

A cohesive approach ensures compliance with laws and regulations: the old, the new and the confusing ones. As a team united, they can help get the correct definitions and build a well-designed path to success.

Fraud Prevention and Detection

Collaboration enhances the organization's ability to prevent and detect fraud by creating a unified front where information flows seamlessly across departments. When teams—such as internal audit, external audit, compliance, and management—work closely together, they can identify red flags earlier and respond more swiftly to suspicious activities. This collective vigilance not only strengthens controls but also fosters a culture of integrity, making it harder for fraudulent behavior to take root and thrive within the organization.

Operational Efficiency

Unified efforts lead to more efficient operations. When teams align and collaborate seamlessly, their unified efforts eliminate redundancies and streamline processes, leading to smoother workflows and faster decision-making. This synergy allows resources to be used more effectively, reducing costs and minimizing bottlenecks. Ultimately, a coordinated approach drives productivity and empowers the organization to achieve its goals with greater speed and precision.

Without the work of auditors, the audit committee would struggle to gain the knowledge needed to attest to the accuracy of financial statements. Despite being tasked with ensuring financial statements, audit committee members may not have audit experience themselves. This is where the power of a cohesive team comes into play!

Looping in ERM and Corporate Compliance

There are more battalions audit committee can rely on to face battle more effectively. The audit committee can rely on Enterprise Risk Management (ERM) and Corporate Compliance to enhance their oversight and governance functions. ERM provides a holistic approach to managing risks, ensuring all significant risks are identified and managed effectively. Corporate Compliance ensures adherence to laws, regulations, and internal policies, protecting the organization from legal risks and enhancing its reputation.

By leveraging ERM and Corporate Compliance, the audit committee can enhance their ability to oversee financial reporting, manage risks, ensure compliance with laws and regulations, and prevent and detect fraud. This unified approach leads to more efficient operations and builds stakeholder confidence in the organization's governance and financial integrity.

> The audit committee is the board's compass and conscience, keeping the organization true to its course and its values.

The tasks of the audit committee are enormous, but by relying on "their village"—internal audit, external audit, ERM, and corporate compliance—the audit committee can delegate tasks and ensure a thorough allocation of duties. This unified approach leads to more efficient operations and builds stakeholder confidence in the organization's governance and financial integrity.

The audit committee isn't a mystery—it's the lighthouse guiding truth through fog.

4

Voices from the Watchtower

External Assurance and Shared Accountability

THE STRENGTH OF THE TEAM IS EACH INDIVIDUAL MEMBER. THE STRENGTH OF EACH MEMBER IS THE TEAM.

—PHIL JACKSON

Imagine the audit committee as the ship's bridge—steady, strategic, and vital to keeping the vessel on course. Composition and structure are the crew manifest and deck design that make smooth sailing possible. The right mix of expertise, experience, and independence ensures that when the waters grow choppy—be it a financial storm or a governance squall—the committee has the balance and agility to steer wisely. Just as a well-crewed ship cannot rely on a single navigator, a well-structured audit committee thrives on diverse minds, clearly defined roles, and shared accountability that keep the enterprise from drifting off course. The normal composition of an audit committee typically includes the following elements.

Independence

Members of the audit committee need to be as independent as a lone wolf on the hunt—untethered from management's daily hustle to deliver sharp, unbiased oversight. Their role demands a clear, unclouded lens, free from the fog of personal or financial entanglements that could blur judgment or invite conflicts of interest. Think of it this way: you

DOI: 10.1201/9781003642398-4

wouldn't want the gatekeeper to have a secret handshake with the very folks they're meant to scrutinize.

This independence isn't just a nice-to-have; it's the bedrock of trust, the invisible armor that shields the committee's integrity. That means committee members should steer clear of significant financial stakes in the company—and absolutely avoid sitting on the audit committee of a competitor, where loyalties could be divided and confidential strategies inadvertently exposed. They will be privy to a wealth of confidential information and though trusted to maintain that confidentiality, any hinderances or temptations are best avoided.

In essence, independence is the audit committee's superpower. Without it, oversight risks becoming a game of blindfolded darts—messy, risky, and downright avoidable.

Financial Expertise

At least one member of the audit committee should be the financial wizard in the room—the person who reads financial statements like a gripping novel and sees beyond the numbers to the story they tell. This individual isn't just number-savvy; they possess a deep, intuitive grasp of accounting principles and auditing standards, turning complex financial jargon into clear, actionable insight.

Think of this expert as the committee's financial compass—the steady hand that navigates through balance sheets, income statements, and cash flow mysteries with confidence and precision. Their expertise transforms raw data into a strategic asset, spotting red flags, uncovering hidden risks, and ensuring the numbers don't just add up, but add meaning.

Picking the right financial expert for the audit committee isn't just a checkbox exercise—it's a strategic move that can make or break the whole oversight game. Their qualifications aren't just credentials on paper; they're the foundation for sharp financial storytelling, savvy risk spotting, and keeping compliance tight. Getting this right means the committee can confidently steer through complex reports and murky numbers without losing sight of the bigger picture.

Here are some key qualifications.

Thorough Understanding of Financial Statements

Financial experts should possess a deep understanding of financial statements, including balance sheets, income statements, and cash flow statements. This knowledge enables them to effectively oversee the financial reporting process and ensure accuracy and reliability.

Knowledge of Accounting Principles and Auditing Standards

Financial experts should be well-versed in accounting principles and auditing standards. This expertise allows them to evaluate the adequacy of internal controls, assess financial risks, and ensure compliance with relevant regulations. They do not need to be formal CPAs or equivalents but they should feel comfortable reading and analyzing financial statements. If they are versed in ratio analysts, all the better, but not necessary to meet compliance.

Experience in Financial Oversight

Financial experts should have experience in financial oversight, such as serving in roles like Chief Financial Officer (CFO), Controller, or similar positions. This experience equips them with the skills needed to scrutinize financial data and transactions, identify potential red flags, and prevent and detect fraudulent activities.

They should be confident about their knowledge and question items that appear suspicious or require further qualifications. It is one thing to have these experiences, they should be able to prove their skill based on their performance.

Ability to Assess Risk Management Processes

Financial experts should be capable of identifying and assessing financial risks. Their expertise allows them to evaluate the effectiveness of risk management processes and ensure that the organization is well-prepared to handle potential financial challenges.

Commitment to Continuous Learning

Financial experts, and for that matter all members of the committee, should be committed to continuous learning and staying informed about new accounting standards, regulatory changes, and industry best practices. This commitment ensures that they remain effective in their roles and can adapt to evolving responsibilities.

Focus on Independence

Financial experts should be independent of the company's management to ensure unbiased oversight. This independence is crucial for maintaining the integrity and effectiveness of the audit committee.

Without this financial anchor, the committee risks sailing blind in choppy waters, vulnerable to misinterpretation or oversight. So, having at least one member fluent in the language of finance isn't just recommended—it's mission critical.

Diversity

Diversity on an audit committee isn't just a box to tick or a line on a corporate résumé—it's the secret sauce that transforms ordinary oversight into extraordinary insight. When we talk about diversity, we're peeling back layers far beyond gender or ethnicity. It's about weaving together a rich tapestry of perspectives, experiences, and ways of thinking that challenge groupthink and spark fresh ideas.

Imagine a room where backgrounds range from finance gurus to tech innovators, from seasoned risk warriors to sharp-eyed storytellers. Each member brings their own lens—shaped by culture, education, career twists, and even life's curveballs—that uncovers blind spots others might miss. This kaleidoscope of viewpoints supercharges the committee's ability to sniff out risks lurking in corners often overlooked and to tackle challenges with creativity and courage.

> In essence, diversity is the committee's radar and rocket fuel—helping them not just see more clearly but also soar higher.

It's about inviting the uncomfortable questions, welcoming constructive tension, and turning differences into a powerhouse of problem-solving. Because when a committee truly embraces diversity, it doesn't just check a box—it elevates the entire governance game.

Relevant Skill Sets

Members of the audit committee should be a carefully curated blend of talents—a powerhouse cocktail of skills and expertise tailored to the company's unique industry and operational heartbeat. This isn't a one-size-fits-all gig; it's more like assembling an elite squad where each member brings their own specialty to the war room.

You want risk whisperers who can sniff out trouble before it arrives, compliance champions who know the rulebook inside out (and when to challenge it), guardians of internal controls who make sure the gears don't grind, and corporate governance gurus who keep the ethical compass spinning true north. Together, they form a dynamic ecosystem, a living, breathing think tank that can dissect complexity with surgical precision and craft solutions that aren't just safe—but smart.

This mix of expertise fuels smarter oversight, sharper questions, and a deeper understanding of the business's twists and turns. It's the difference between steering a ship through familiar waters and navigating the stormy seas of today's volatile markets. When audit committees get their mix right, they don't just manage risk—they own it, tame it, and turn it into opportunity.

Commitment and Availability

Audit committee members must come to the table with more than just good intentions—they need real commitment, matched with the time and availability to dive deep into their responsibilities. This isn't a part-time gig you can tick off between emails or squeeze in between meetings. It demands presence, preparation, and proactive engagement.

They need to show up—not just physically, but mentally—at every meeting, ready to challenge, question, and collaborate. It means rolling up their sleeves to pour over financial reports, audit findings, risk assessments, and compliance updates, often outside of scheduled meetings. Staying current isn't optional; it's essential. The landscape shifts fast—from new regulations to emerging risks—so members must stay informed and ahead of the curve.

As we highlighted back in Chapter 1, this commitment stretches far beyond the familiar rhythm of quarterly meetings. It's about living the role—being accessible for ad hoc discussions, dedicating time to ongoing education, and engaging with management, auditors, and fellow committee members whenever the organization's integrity calls for it. In today's fast-paced, risk-filled world, effective audit committee service requires energy, focus, and a hunger for continuous learning.

Having a diverse audit committee brings numerous benefits to an organization. Some advantages are as follows.

Enhanced Perspectives

A diverse audit committee brings a range of perspectives and experiences to the table. This diversity can enhance the committee's ability to identify and address various risks and challenges, leading to more comprehensive and effective oversight.

Different viewpoints can stimulate critical thinking and innovative solutions, helping the audit committee make well-informed decisions.

Increased Credibility and Trust

A diverse audit committee can enhance the credibility and trust of stakeholders, including shareholders, lenders, and regulatory authorities. Stakeholders are more likely to trust the financial statements and governance practices of an organization with a diverse and knowledgeable audit committee.

Better Risk Management

Diversity in the audit committee can improve risk management by bringing different perspectives on potential risks and their mitigation. This can lead to a more robust risk management framework.

Enhanced Compliance and Governance

A diverse audit committee is better equipped to ensure compliance with laws and regulations. Members with different backgrounds and expertise can provide valuable insights into the impact of new accounting standards and regulatory changes on the organization's financial reporting and internal controls.

Strengthened Stakeholder Relationships

A diverse audit committee can help build stronger relationships with stakeholders by demonstrating a commitment to inclusivity and representation. This can enhance the organization's reputation and foster a culture of trust and accountability.

Chairing an Audit Committee

The Chair of the Audit Committee plays a pivotal role in ensuring the effectiveness and efficiency of the committee's operations. Here are some key responsibilities and best practices for chairing an audit committee.

Leadership and Coordination

The Chair leads the audit committee, setting the agenda for meetings, and ensuring that all members are well-prepared to discuss the issues at hand. They coordinate with internal and external auditors, management, and other stakeholders to ensure that the committee's activities are aligned with the organization's objectives. They may be tasked to provide training or allowing committee members to attend training within the auspices of their established operating budget. They should be well experienced and willing in speaking to stakeholders with elegance and professionalism.

Understanding of the Internal Audit Charter

The Chair should have a thorough understanding of the internal audit charter, which outlines the purpose, authority, and responsibility of the internal audit function. This knowledge helps the Chairman guide the committee in overseeing the internal audit process effectively. At the same token he (or she) should be just as well versed in the understanding of the audit committee charter.

The external auditor doesn't just confirm the view—they steady the lens through which integrity is seen.

5

The Moral Compass at Work

Charting Compliance with a True Captain

THE PRICE OF GREATNESS IS RESPONSIBILITY.
—WINSTON CHURCHILL

The primary purpose of the audit committee charter is to define the committee's oversight responsibilities, particularly regarding financial reporting, internal controls, risk management, compliance, and the relationship with internal and external auditors.

Key Components

Authority and Composition

The charter specifies the audit committee's authority granted by the board of directors, including its composition, independence requirements, and qualifications of its members.

The charter also clarifies the reporting structure of the audit committee, indicating to whom the committee is accountable and the extent of its decision-making authority. It may delineate procedures for escalating significant issues to the board and outline expectations for confidentiality and integrity in carrying out committee functions. Additionally, the charter can specify succession planning and the process for appointing new committee members to ensure consistent oversight and continuity.

DOI: 10.1201/9781003642398-5

Responsibilities

The charter details the committee's main duties, such as overseeing financial reporting, reviewing internal controls, monitoring risk management processes, and ensuring compliance with laws and regulations. Beyond these core responsibilities, the audit committee charter may also address how the committee interacts with other board committees and management, ensuring a coordinated approach to corporate governance. The charter can establish protocols for the committee to access independent advice or resources when needed, thereby strengthening its oversight capabilities and supporting informed decision-making.

Auditor Relations

It sets forth the committee's duties in selecting, evaluating, and communicating with external auditors, as well as overseeing the internal audit function.

Meetings and Reporting

The charter defines the frequency of meetings, required attendees, and procedures for regular reporting to the board of directors. It may also speak as to what constitutes a quorum, advanced notification requirements, and method of meeting (Zoom, phone, live, etc.).

Review and Assessment

It includes guidelines for annual performance reviews of the committee and periodic updates to the charter itself.

Regulatory Requirements

USA

In the United States, public company audit committees are subject to rules and regulations set by the Securities and Exchange Commission (SEC) and stock exchanges such as the New York Stock Exchange (NYSE) and National Association of Securities Dealers Automated Quotations (NASDAQ). These regulations require companies to maintain a written audit committee charter that addresses the committee's scope, membership, and processes.

The audit committee charter is a public document (for listed companies) and is often included in the company's proxy statement or corporate governance section of its website. It demonstrates the company's commitment to robust oversight, transparency, and accountability—key pillars in maintaining stakeholder trust and regulatory compliance.

Europe

European Union

The European Union's directives on statutory audits require public-interest entities (including listed companies, banks, and insurance companies) to establish an audit committee or a similar body. The responsibilities and composition are outlined in the EU Audit Directive (2014/56/EU) and Regulation (EU) No 537/2014. While not always called a "charter," companies must document the committee's functions, independence, and qualifications in accordance with national transpositions of these directives. Corporate governance codes, such as the U.K. Corporate Governance Code and Germany's Deutscher Corporate Governance Kodex, also require written terms of reference, which function similarly to U.S. audit committee charters.

United Kingdom

In the United Kingdom, companies listed on the London Stock Exchange must comply (or explain non-compliance) with the U.K. Corporate Governance Code, which requires an audit committee with clearly defined written terms of reference. These terms cover membership, roles, responsibilities, and reporting—essentially mirroring the function of a U.S. audit committee charter.

Germany

German listed companies follow the provisions of the German Corporate Governance Code, which encourages the formation of audit committees with written rules of procedure. These documents, while sometimes less prescriptive than U.S. charters, fulfill a similar role in defining the committee's scope and authority.

Australia

The Australian Stock Exchanges' Corporate Governance Council's Principles and Recommendations require listed entities to have an audit committee and to disclose its charter. This charter must specify the committee's role, composition, operation, and authority, aligning closely with U.S. practice.

For the ease of reading and writing this book, the term Audit Charter is used; it should be taken as the U.S. audit charter or equivalent document in the international marketplace.

Effective Communication

The Chair facilitates open and transparent communication among committee members, management, and auditors. This includes ensuring that all relevant information is shared and discussed, and that any concerns or issues are addressed promptly.

Oversight of Financial Reporting and Internal Controls

The Chair ensures that the audit committee effectively oversees the financial reporting process and internal controls. This includes reviewing financial statements, assessing the adequacy of internal controls, and ensuring compliance with relevant laws and regulations.

Risk Management and Compliance Monitoring

The Chair plays a crucial role in overseeing the organization's risk management and compliance efforts. This includes ensuring that the organization has robust risk management processes in place and that it complies with all applicable laws and regulations.

Interaction with Internal and External Auditors

The Chair ensures that the audit committee maintains a productive relationship with both internal and external auditors. This includes overseeing the selection and evaluation of auditors, reviewing audit plans and reports, and ensuring that any audit findings are addressed appropriately.

> The audit committee chair—the captain of the ship, the maestro of the oversight orchestra, the one who turns a room full of experts into a powerhouse of clarity and action is a powerful position.

Chairing an audit committee is less about wielding a gavel and more about wielding influence with finesse, diplomacy, wisdom, and a splash of charisma. So, what does that look like in practice?

Own the Room, Without Owning the Conversation

A great chair sets the tone—inviting voices, encouraging questions, and making sure no insight goes unheard. They're the ultimate conductor, keeping rhythm without drowning out soloists. That means mastering the art of listening as much as leading, knowing when to press, when to pause, and when to pivot. They should understand when a committee member is being silent and determine whether this silence is voluntary or if the member is being coerced by another member or an external force. They should understand the powers of team dynamics to ensure that all voices are equal—new and experienced members alike.

Master the Agenda, But Stay Flexible

The chair crafts a sharp, purposeful agenda that tackles the pressing issues with laser focus. But life isn't scripted, and neither are meetings. A savvy chair knows how to pivot when the unexpected surfaces—balancing structure with spontaneity like a seasoned jazz player.

Be the Bridge Builder

Between internal audit, external audit, management, and the board, the chair is the connector—breaking down silos, building trust, and turning diverse perspectives into collective wisdom. They keep the committee's eyes on the prize while navigating personalities and power dynamics with grace.

Champion Continuous Learning

The chair models curiosity and growth, pushing the committee to stay sharp on emerging risks, new regulations, and innovative audit techniques. It's about setting a culture where learning isn't an afterthought but the heartbeat of effective oversight.

Drive Accountability without Drama

They ensure actions get done—not by wielding authority, but by inspiring responsibility and follow-through. The chair holds the committee accountable, keeping momentum alive and making sure recommendations don't gather dust.

How Should the Chair Be Elected or Appointed?

Picking the chair is a big deal—like casting the lead in a play that defines the company's governance narrative.

Independent First

The chair should be an independent director—someone free from management ties to keep oversight unbiased and sharp.

Financial Fluency

Bonus points if they bring strong financial expertise to the table, but they don't have to be a CPA or CFO; they just need to understand the language of numbers well enough to steer the ship confidently.

Peer Selection

Ideally, the committee members elect their chair democratically—because who better to judge leadership ability than the team itself? This also builds respect and buy-in from day one. Transparency in the selection process is crucial. The criteria, procedures, and rationale for choosing the chair should be clearly communicated to all stakeholders, ensuring trust and clarity throughout. This openness helps to minimize potential conflicts and supports a healthy governance culture.

Board Ratification

The full board should formally approve the choice, reinforcing the chair's authority and underscoring the governance commitment at the highest level. Whomever is tasked with overseeing the nomination should ensure that the selection is based on experience, not just a popularity contest.

Term Limits

To keep energy fresh and perspectives vibrant, consider reasonable term limits with options for renewal. Too long, and complacency creeps in; too short, and momentum stalls. Options for renewal keep commitment in check.

The audit committee chair isn't just a title—it's a responsibility charged with curiosity, courage, and connection. The right chair can transform oversight from a chore into a strategic powerhouse.

So, if selected, how do you become this powerhouse?

First and foremost, the Chair is the cultural catalyst of the audit committee.

> A good Chair signals that transparency, integrity, and independence aren't buzzwords—they're table stakes.

They foster an atmosphere where committee members, management, and auditors feel empowered to speak up, challenge assumptions, and dig deeper.

Pro tip: Lead with curiosity, not criticism. Ask thoughtful questions. Model constructive dissent. Be firm on expectations, flexible in style.

Next, remember that time is a precious commodity—don't let it be squandered. An efficient Chair shapes the agenda like a sculptor, focusing on what matters most: high-risk areas, complex judgments, and strategic foresight. Routine updates? Summarize and circulate in advance.

Power move: Work with the internal auditor, external auditor, and CFO *before* the meeting to prioritize discussion items. Leave breathing room for red flags and emergent issues.

The best Chairs are not just good at oversight—they're students of change. They keep a keen eye on emerging risks: AI, cybersecurity, ESG disclosures, whistleblower trends, regulatory shifts. They also understand enough audit/accounting detail to ask pointed questions—without stepping into operational quicksand.

Stay sharp: Regularly meet with internal audit, external auditors, and compliance heads outside of meetings. Subscribe to alerts. Attend briefings. Read the room *and* the regulations. Ask questions where and whenever possible. While we are generally open and accommodating, this is a moment that calls for discernment and resolve rather than default acceptance.

Play Connect the Dots: Internal Audit, External Audit, Management, Legal, Risk—the Chair's job is to connect the dots, not fence them off. Act as a liaison, not a gatekeeper. Make sure everyone's rowing in the same direction, without compromising independence.

Golden thread—facilitate a triangular relationship: management provides data, Internal Audit offers insight, and External Audit gives perspective. Your role? Weave those threads into a meaningful tapestry.

A great Chair knows their team—their strengths, blind spots, and bandwidth. They also honestly assess for weaknesses. They make sure the committee has the right skills (e.g., tech fluency, sector expertise, financial literacy) and that each voice is heard. A great leader will also bolster the skills of their team, building his or her replacement.

Smart strategy: Rotate roles to keep minds fresh. Foster peer-to-peer accountability. Encourage continuing education—and lead by example.

The audit committee is not a courtroom or a classroom—it's a decision-driving body. The Chair ensures that key issues raised are tracked, actioned, and resolved. Audit findings? Assign owners. Deadlines? Lock them in. Gaps in control or reporting? Get a timeline for remediation.

Efficiency trick: Use dashboards or action logs to monitor progress. Each meeting should build upon the last, not reset the clock. If need be, ask audit to create dashboards for the team.

The Chair must be the clear, credible voice to the Board. What does the Board need to know? What keeps the board up at night? What keeps the Audit Committee up at night? What's working well? How can they make things easier? What secrets is the organization keeping from the board? Is the board operating with a current playbook, or are its methods and ideologies old and stale?

Think like a storyteller: Use plain language, not audit jargon. Elevate insight, not just information. Champion the function's value, especially when things go right—not just when they go wrong. If items ae being disclosed in manners that the committee finds confusing, ask the report writers for clarity and potential future changes.

Sometimes, a Chair has to hold the line. When there's pressure to "gloss over" an issue, downplay a risk, or rush a decision, the Chair must protect the process and the principle. That's the job. Not the most glamorous part, but perhaps the most important.

In short, an effective Audit Committee Chair is part mentor, part maestro balancing, scrutiny with support, structure with flexibility, and compliance with courage. When the Chair is sharp, prepared, and principled, the whole organization benefits. It's not just about keeping the auditors honest, it's about helping the enterprise thrive in complexity, not just survive it.

The Audit Committee needs to understand the role of the Internal Audit Charter. An audit committee that doesn't understand the internal audit charter is like a captain who's never read the ship's navigation chart; eventually, you're going to run aground. The internal audit charter may not look like much at first glance, often just a few tidy pages, but in reality, it's the heartbeat of the internal audit function. It defines the mission, the scope, and the authority of internal audit within the organization. For an audit committee, understanding this document is not optional; it's foundational. You can't oversee what you don't understand, and you certainly can't defend a function if you haven't grasped the blueprint it's meant to follow. The charter sets the rules of engagement between internal audit, management, and the board, and it's the audit committee's job to make sure those rules are clear, relevant, and lived out in practice.

Too often, the charter becomes a "file-and-forget" artifact, reviewed when the internal audit function is first set up, then quietly gathering digital dust. It may make an appearance, now and again, at audit staff meetings but it is a living, breathing document and needs to be treated as such. The audit committee must resist the temptation to draft, display, and die. A stagnant charter can suffocate an otherwise capable audit team, leaving them unclear on their mandate or, worse, vulnerable to being steered away from sensitive areas. An engaged audit committee treats the charter as a living document; revisiting it annually, ensuring it reflects the organization's current risks, regulatory environment, and strategic objectives. They bring audit in to hear their thoughts on the charter.

Understanding the charter also means appreciating its role as a shield for internal audit's independence. The document should clearly state that internal audit reports functionally to the audit committee, not management, and that it has unfettered access to the information, people, and systems it needs to do its work. When internal audit bumps up against resistance, perhaps from an overprotective executive or a nervous department head, the audit committee becomes the backstop. Without a clear charter to point to, those battles are harder to win.

The audit committee's responsibilities go beyond simply "approving" the charter. They need to read it with a critical eye: Does it clearly define the scope of internal audit's work? Does it align with the International Standards for the Professional Practice of Internal Auditing? Does it explicitly protect the function's right to report findings without fear of reprisal? A vague or poorly worded charter is an open invitation for scope creep, confusion, or deliberate obstruction. The committee's role is to close those gaps before they become real-world problems.

There's also a strategic dimension. The charter is not just about compliance; it's about positioning internal audit as a value creator, not just a fault finder. An astute audit committee will ensure the charter empowers internal audit to look beyond traditional financial and compliance audits, giving it the remit to assess operational efficiency, emerging risks, and even organizational culture. In other words, the charter should give internal audit permission to go where the real risks live, even if those areas are politically sensitive.

Training and awareness play a role too. New audit committee members, particularly those without a background in governance or auditing, need to be brought up to speed on what the charter says and why it matters. The most effective committees treat this as part of their onboarding process, ensuring every member can confidently explain internal audit's role to anyone who asks. After all, if the committee doesn't understand the function it oversees, how can it credibly defend its budget, its priorities, or its independence?

Finally, the audit committee must ensure that the charter is more than just words on a page—it needs to be reflected in daily operations. That means checking that internal audit is working to the scope defined, that management respects the boundaries set, and that the function's reporting lines remain intact. It's not enough to review the charter in January and forget about it until next year. Oversight is an ongoing act of vigilance, and the audit committee is the one holding the flashlight. The charter isn't paperwork; it's a promise. And an audit committee that guards that promise turns internal audit from a department into a force.

> When the right people sit in the right seats, with clear lines of authority and purpose, the audit committee becomes more than a structure; it becomes the keel of the ship, holding the course steady no matter how fierce the storm.

The composition and structure of the audit committee are the architecture of trust. Choose the wrong materials and the frame will splinter when the first gust of crisis hits. Choose wisely and you build a structure that can carry the full weight of accountability, weather the tempests of scrutiny, and stand as a visible symbol of integrity. When the right people sit in the right seats, with clarity of role and strength of purpose, the audit committee becomes more than a governance requirement; it becomes the lighthouse that guides the organization safely through uncertain waters.

> A strong committee is like a well-built bridge—it doesn't creak under pressure; it flexes with grace.

Bridging management and internal audit is not a single crossing but a continuous voyage. The audit committee stands as the ship's unshakable compass, aligning management's ambition with audit's insight and keeping the corporate vessel steady even when winds shift or tides surprise. When curiosity replaces jargon, when brevity sharpens focus, and when every voice can speak without fear, the river between risk and opportunity becomes not a barrier but a bright thoroughfare of trust.

And so the chapter closes with a gentle wake on open water: management, internal audit, and the audit committee sailing in concert, sails trimmed and eyes on the stars.

Their partnership is the keel that keeps the organization upright, the chart that plots safe passage, and the bridge that spans every current. With clarity as their sextant and integrity as their North Star, they steer together toward a horizon of growth, resilience, and lasting credibility.

6
The Conscience of the Board
Why Oversight Matters More than Ever

LEADERSHIP IS NOT ABOUT BEING IN CHARGE. IT IS ABOUT TAKING CARE OF THOSE IN YOUR CHARGE.

—SIMON SINEK

An audit committee's true power lies not in authority, but in the courage to question, the discipline to listen, and the wisdom to act in the best interests of those they serve. It ties leadership, oversight, and fiduciary responsibility into one neat package, without sounding like a dusty corporate manual. It is a living and breathing entity and should be seen and heard. An effective audit committee is both anchor and compass steadying the ship while pointing it toward safe, ethical waters.

Financial Reporting Oversight

Financial reporting oversight is the audit committee's watchtower duty—perched high enough to see the full landscape, sharp-eyed enough to spot trouble before it reaches the gates. It's not about writing the financial story—that's management's pen—but about making sure the tale told is accurate, complete, and worthy of trust. The committee pores over the draft financial statements, testing the numbers, poking at the estimates, and asking the questions that make creative accounting break into a sweat. They sit across from the external auditors, digging into findings, sniffing out red flags, and making sure independence isn't just a word in the audit plan.

DOI: 10.1201/9781003642398-6

They keep a wary eye on the systems and controls that guard against errors and fraud, knowing that one weak link can unravel the whole chain. And through it all, they carry the unshakable knowledge that every investor, regulator, donor, and stakeholder is counting on them to keep the story straight.

If management is the author, the audit committee is the relentless proofreader—checking every comma, verifying every plot twist, and ensuring that no fiction sneaks into the facts. In their hands, oversight isn't a box to tick; it's the front line of trust.

Financial reporting oversight also means standing guard over the process itself, not just the end product. The audit committee has to understand how the numbers are born—how transactions are captured, processed, and translated into the language of accounting. If the machinery behind the reporting creaks or stutters, the committee needs to hear it, see it, and fix it before it turns into a scandal splashed across the headlines. They don't operate in the shadows; their presence is a quiet but constant signal to management that the reporting process is under active, intelligent scrutiny.

It's also about timing. Financial reporting doesn't happen in a leisurely stroll—it's a sprint to the deadline. Under pressure, mistakes multiply and corners tend to be cut. The audit committee ensures that speed never sacrifices substance. They push for processes that can withstand the crunch without losing accuracy or depth, knowing that rushed numbers are dangerous numbers. In their world, "close enough" is never good enough.

Relationships matter too. A committee that merely ticks boxes will miss what a committee that builds trust can catch. The most effective members forge working relationships with finance teams, internal auditors, and external auditors alike—relationships that allow for frank discussions, early warnings, and the sharing of uncomfortable truths. They are approachable without being lenient, authoritative without being authoritarian. People talk to them because they listen, and they listen because they care about getting it right.

They also have to be alert to the tone at the top. Financial reporting is shaped not just by rules but by culture. If leadership winks at aggressive accounting or tolerates "interpretive flexibility" when numbers are inconvenient, the audit committee must step in. They are the cultural counterweight, the ones who remind everyone that transparency is not a luxury—it's the price of credibility. This means challenging management when necessary, even if it makes for tense conversations and awkward boardroom silences.

Then there's the duty to see beyond the present. Oversight isn't just about the year-end figures; it's about spotting patterns, trends, and future risks. Is the organization venturing into riskier markets? Is the business model changing in ways that make revenue recognition trickier? Are regulatory shifts on the horizon that could reshape disclosure requirements? The committee has to think like chess players, seeing several moves ahead, so the financial reporting process doesn't stumble into tomorrow's traps.

And, perhaps most importantly, financial reporting oversight is about protecting the invisible currency—trust.

> Trust is what gives numbers their power. Without it, even the most carefully prepared statements are just ink on paper.

The audit committee's work may never trend on social media, but it quietly underwrites the organization's credibility in the eyes of those who matter most. It's the kind of work that only gets noticed when it fails—which is precisely why the best committees make sure it never does.

In the end, financial reporting oversight is less about spreadsheets and more about stewardship. It's the quiet courage to ask the awkward question, the persistence to dig one layer deeper, the conviction to hold the line when pressure mounts. An audit committee that takes this role seriously becomes more than a checkpoint in the process—it becomes the conscience of the numbers. And in a world where trust can evaporate in a headline, that conscience may be the most valuable asset an organization owns.

Financial reporting oversight never exists in isolation. It is built on the scaffolding of legislation, regulation, and governance codes that, while differing in detail across countries, share a common heartbeat; the preservation of trust in the numbers. In the United States, the Sarbanes–Oxley Act of 2002 transformed the landscape, making audit committees directly responsible for overseeing the external audit, ensuring the independence of the auditors, and safeguarding the accuracy and completeness of financial disclosures.

In the United Kingdom, the Corporate Governance Code demands that boards establish transparent and rigorous arrangements for monitoring risk and financial reporting. The European Union's Audit Directive sets similar expectations, as do Australia's Corporations Act, Canada's Canadian Securities Administrators' rules, and the King IV Code of Governance in South Africa. The legislative language may vary, yet the central truth is universal; the audit committee is the sentry at the gate of transparency, charged with making sure that the information leaving the organization is both truthful and timely.

Legislation not only outlines the duties of the audit committee; it also determines where it sits in the organizational hierarchy. This placement is deliberate.

> If the fox cannot guard the henhouse, then management cannot be the ultimate overseer of its own reporting.

For this reason, laws and governance codes place oversight responsibility in the hands of independent, non-executive directors who report to the full board and, through the board, to shareholders or other primary stakeholders. This structure provides the necessary distance between those who prepare the financial statements and those who ensure those statements tell the unvarnished truth.

In reality, organizational hierarchies are not always so clean. In some companies, management attempts to filter or pre-screen the information that reaches the audit committee, softening the edges or removing details that may cause discomfort. In others, reporting lines for finance and assurance functions are so tangled that true accountability is lost in the maze. This is where an experienced audit committee chair and well-informed members become essential. They must insist on unfiltered access to the Chief Financial Officer, to the external auditors, and to anyone whose input is necessary to form an accurate understanding of the organization's financial position. The committee must hear the truth before it is polished into a corporate narrative.

In the ideal structure, the audit committee reports directly to the full board of directors or trustees, with its chair maintaining an open and direct channel to the board chair. This reporting line ensures that the committee's insights and concerns are heard at the highest level without distortion. The Chief Financial Officer and the Chief Executive Officer attend audit committee meetings by invitation, contributing to the dialogue but never acting as gatekeepers of information. The external auditor has both the right and the obligation to meet privately with the audit committee, providing a candid view of the financial reporting process without the presence of management.

The organizational hierarchy should also give the audit committee functional oversight of the internal audit function. The Chief Audit Executive should report administratively to the Chief Executive Officer for day-to-day operations, yet functionally to the audit committee for all matters of substance. This dual reporting relationship preserves internal audit's independence while ensuring that its work remains aligned with the strategic direction of the organization. It also provides a direct path for escalating concerns about financial reporting, preventing such concerns from being buried under political pressure or internal resistance.

Legislation and governance codes are designed to prevent structural weaknesses, but they can only go so far. True strength comes when the audit committee actively embraces best practice, going beyond the letter of the law. A well-structured hierarchy, backed by legal authority, transforms the audit committee from a passive reviewer of reports into an empowered guardian of financial integrity. In the complex reality of organizational life, hierarchies can be manipulated, reporting lines can blur, and access to information can be subtly restricted. In the ideal world, these lines are drawn clearly, enforced consistently, and defended vigorously.

This clarity of structure matters because trust is fragile.

The moment reporting lines are compromised or access to information is denied, the entire oversight framework is weakened. Legislation sets the minimum standard, but the best audit committees aim far higher. They understand that financial reporting oversight is not about doing the bare minimum to comply with the rules; it is about creating the conditions in which the truth can always rise to the surface, unaltered and undistorted.

> Legislation sets the floor, but structure holds the line. The right hierarchy gives the audit committee the power to keep the truth intact.

Legislation may set the floor for financial reporting oversight, but structure sets the strength. Laws and governance codes place the audit committee high in the organizational hierarchy to keep it independent from management and directly accountable to the board. In the ideal design, the committee has unfiltered access to the Chief Financial Officer, the external auditors, and the Chief Audit Executive, who reports administratively to the Chief Executive Officer yet functionally to the committee. This clarity of line and authority allows the audit committee to act as the uncompromised guardian of financial integrity, ensuring that the truth in the numbers cannot be diluted before it reaches those who need to know.

Risk Management and Compliance Monitoring

The audit committee stands at the threshold where risk meets responsibility, its gaze sweeping across both compliance and emerging threats. In a world where risk no longer knocks politely but barrels through the door, the audit committee is the vigilant sentinel that ensures no storm arrives unannounced.

Legislation codifies this role. U.S. listing rules demand that audit committees oversee risk and compliance as much as financial reporting; European directives require them to monitor internal controls and risk management systems as part of their core charter. These legal frameworks position audit committees not as passive monitors, but as active architects of integrity.

Within the corporate architecture, the audit committee is the roof and the compass. It watches over compliance with laws and regulations, ensuring that the organization respects the boundaries within which it must operate. From anti-corruption statutes and data privacy mandates to industry-specific obligations, the audit committee ensures that compliance is not a checklist but a culture.

At the same time, it confronts risk in all its guises. It listens as compliance officers, internal audit, and legal counsel report emerging threats, from cyber vulnerabilities to reputational chasms, ensuring that whispers in the hallways rise into boardroom dialogue. When risk is evolving faster than plans can be written, the audit committee must be not only watching the future but shaping how the organization prepares for it.

Richard F. Chambers is the former President and CEO of The Institute of Internal Auditors (IIA), where he served from 2009 to 2021. He's widely respected for his thought leadership in internal auditing, risk management, and governance. I was listening to Mr. Chambers talk and he hit the nails on the head. He stated risk management "can no longer be a once-a-year process" in this era of permacrisis. That phrase should resonate in every boardroom; for the audit committee, the challenge is to keep risk front and center! It should not be a seasonal headline but a steady hum in every discussion.

Mr. Chambers said: Internal audit must take a more continuous approach to risk assessment. Audit plans and coverage should constantly evolve as new, potential risks surface and undergo assessment.

All this can be found on his Blog—Audit Beacon. Of particular importance is the blog of July 31, 2014—Auditing at the Speed of Risk.

The blog entry "Auditing at the Speed of Risk" emphasizes the necessity for audit committees and internal audit functions to adopt a more agile, continuous approach to risk management.

In today's environment, characterized by a constant stream of new and evolving threats, the blog argues that risk assessment can no longer remain a once-a-year exercise. Instead, both the audit committee and internal audit must keep risk at the forefront, integrating it into regular boardroom discussions and ensuring audit plans are always evolving to address emerging challenges.

The piece highlights the importance of proactive risk identification and remediation, advocating for dynamic risk dashboards and ongoing dialogue rather than static, periodic updates. It also stresses that compliance should be embedded into the organizational culture, with audit committees acting as guardians of both compliance and integrity. The blog underscores the need for internal audit to be courageous and collaborative, mapping blind spots and surfacing risks before they materialize, thereby transforming risk management from a procedural activity into a continuous strategic priority. Though this blog was written many years ago, the truth still bellows through to today.

To keep pace with shifting risk, audit committees must foster continuous dialogue, not sporadic updates. They must demand dynamic risk dashboards, not static slides, so they can see risks emerging, evolving, and ideally being neutralized in real time. Audit Committee meetings and documentation should include risks in the waters ahead and the contingencies to how to charter troubled waters.

Compliance, then, is not about reacting to what's broken; it's about pre-empting what could break. The audit committee must insist on proactive identification of gaps, then track remediation until risks are no longer "anticipated" but understood and addressed. Compliance is the vaccine for disease, not the medical treatment.

True compliance oversight also involves tone at the top. The audit committee must call out when culture wobbles, observing whether shortcuts in one corner of the business ripple contamination across the enterprise. Compliance must be woven into the organization's DNA, and the audit committee is its guardian.

> The audit committee's power is not in enforcement but in enlightenment. Its true strength lies in turning complexity into clarity, making sure that every risk, every regulation, every emerging threat, is not just reported but contextualized. Imagine driving a car without a speedometer, Audit Committee is that speedometer—use it to avoid dangerous outcomes.

Compliance and risk are not two separate rivers but a branching out of the same current. The audit committee must keep both streams moving in concert, ensuring that neither compliance rigidness nor risk complacency overwhelms governance.

In the end, the audit committee is not a final reviewer but a forward-looking compass—it ensures that the organization navigates with both caution and vision, that risk is not feared but understood, and that compliance is not enforced but embraced.

Internal audit serves as the audit committee's eyes and ears in the labyrinth of risk. It should map blind spots, whisper warnings, and call out when the risk horizon shifts behind closed doors.

When internal audit and the audit committee speak with clarity and candor, they transform risk from abstract concepts into urgent priorities. As Richard Chambers notes, internal audit must be courageous when management holds back information—but also collaborative enough to bring the challenged truths into committee discussions.

Internal audit's oversight of risk is as much instinct as it is process. The committee relies on its reports not just for assurance, but for insight into emerging vulnerabilities, shifting culture, and areas where compliance may falter. When internal audit connects dots others miss, it turns risk from paper into purpose.

Enterprise Risk Management (ERM) and the Audit Committee

ERM is the architecture within which risk and compliance converge. ERM frames risk not as isolated incidents but as interconnected threats and opportunities that can navigate the organization's journey to continuous existence. ERM is a structured process that helps an organization identify, assess, manage, and monitor all the major risks it faces—so it can achieve its goals and avoid surprises.

Think of ERM as a way for a company to look at all the things that could go wrong (or right), from financial risks to cyber threats to reputation issues, and make smart plans to handle them. It's about seeing the big picture of risk, not just focusing on one area.

- ERM looks at risks across the whole organization, not just in one department.
- It helps leaders make better decisions by understanding what could impact success.
- ERM is ongoing—it's not a one-time checklist, but a continuous process.

ERM is like the navigation system on a ship, helping the crew spot storms, rocks, and opportunities ahead.

The audit committee must champion ERM as more than a process, it must be the steward of a living risk ecosystem. It should ensure that risk appetite is defined, strategic risks are surfaced, and that board-level decisions are informed by a holistic risk landscape.

ERM invites the audit committee to think like an orchestra conductor, harmonizing first-line operations, second-line compliance and risk functions, and third-line internal audit into one coordinated effort. Under ERM, the committee ensures that the silos dissolve and that risk speaks with one voice.

In this ERM framework, the audit committee oversees not just the performance of functions, but the alignment of risk with strategy. It asks whether the risk management process is embedded in decision-making, capital allocation, strategic planning, and culture. It also asks whether the process is embedded fairly and consistently so one process, person, function, or department does not have an overwhelming majority or power or responsibility.

> An audit committee committed to ERM doesn't only ask "what happened"; it asks "what could happen" and "what should we do about it" and "what harm can it do".
>
> It transforms risk oversight into risk leadership, guiding the organization through uncertainty rather than pausing at its edges.

As much as audit committee may feel that internal audit or compliance can navigate the risk landscape at its keel better than they can, they must be cautioned. To maintain independence, they must understand that the IIA has looked at 18 processes around ERM. Of those processes, audit can:

- Provide Assurance on ERM Processes: Internal audit evaluates whether ERM frameworks and activities are effective, fit for purpose, and consistent with the organization's risk appetite. This includes assessing risk identification, assessment, mitigation, monitoring, and reporting.
- Independently assess and report on the adequacy and effectiveness of ERM processes. It ensures that risk is not just identified and documented but actively managed and aligned with the organization's strategy and risk appetite.
- Evaluate Integration of Risk Management: Internal audit reviews how well risk management is embedded across business

processes (strategy, capital allocation, operational decisions). It checks whether ERM is an active part of decision-making and not just a compliance exercise.
- Assess Alignment with Strategy: Internal audit examines whether risk management is aligned with strategic objectives, ensuring that key risks (including emerging risks) are considered in planning and execution.
- Identify Gaps and Blind Spots: By applying a risk-based audit approach, internal audit can point out areas where significant risks may not be fully identified or managed, revealing "blind spots" that could be overlooked by management or the board.
- Review and Challenge Risk Appetite Statements: Internal audit can assess the clarity, relevance, and application of risk appetite and tolerance statements, ensuring that organizational boundaries for risk-taking are clearly defined and adhered to.
- Facilitate Risk Awareness and Culture: While internal audit does not own risk or set culture, it can promote risk-awareness by communicating audit findings, trends, and lessons learned, nudging the organization toward better risk-informed behaviors.
- Report to the Audit Committee and Board: Internal audit provides independent, objective reports to the audit committee and board, highlighting significant risk exposures, control weaknesses, and recommendations for improvement.

The IIA allows internal audit to take on advisory or consulting roles in ERM, as long as it does not assume responsibility for risk management decisions. These roles can include:

- Providing advice on ERM frameworks, tools, and best practices
- Facilitating risk workshops or risk identification sessions
- Educating management and staff on risk concepts and the value of ERM
- Acting as an observer in risk committees or working groups

However, internal audit must remain independent, never owning or managing risks, but objectively evaluating and advising.

To preserve independence, the IIA states that internal audit should not:

- Set the risk appetite
- Make or approve risk management decisions
- Own or manage any part of the ERM process outside its own activities

Rather, it should focus on providing objective assurance and insight, ensuring the ERM program is robust and effective.

Internal audit, according to the IIA, is both a sentinel and a strategist within ERM. Its functions span assurance, assessment, and advisory work, all delivered with an independent perspective that supports the audit committee and management. By doing so, internal audit helps transform risk from a compliance requirement into a source of strategic advantage, ensuring ERM is not only a shield against uncertainty but a compass for opportunity.

- Provide Assurance on ERM Processes: Internal audit evaluates whether ERM frameworks and activities are effective, fit for purpose, and consistent with the organization's risk appetite. This includes assessing risk identification, assessment, mitigation, monitoring, and reporting.
- Evaluate Integration of Risk Management: Internal audit reviews how well risk management is embedded across business processes (strategy, capital allocation, operational decisions). It checks whether ERM is an active part of decision-making and not just a compliance exercise.
- Assess Alignment with Strategy: Internal audit examines whether risk management is aligned with strategic objectives, ensuring that key risks (including emerging risks) are considered in planning and execution.
- Identify Gaps and Blind Spots: By applying a risk-based audit approach, internal audit can point out areas where significant risks may not be fully identified or managed, revealing "blind spots" that could be overlooked by management or the board.
- Review and Challenge Risk Appetite Statements: Internal audit can assess the clarity, relevance, and application of risk appetite and tolerance statements, ensuring that organizational boundaries for risk-taking are clearly defined and adhered to.

- Facilitate Risk Awareness and Culture: While internal audit does not own risk or set culture, it can promote risk-awareness by communicating audit findings, trends, and lessons learned, nudging the organization toward better risk-informed behaviors.
- Report to the Audit Committee and Board: Internal audit provides independent, objective reports to the audit committee and board, highlighting significant risk exposures, control weaknesses, and recommendations for improvement.

When audit committee can wrap their arms around what audit can and cannot do to remain compliant, they are better aligned to divide up responsibilities more effectively and efficiently without compromising compliance and independence.

Now remember, Internal Audit is one of the departments that will help steer the ship to its proper destination. It can still utilize other parties to help then. There is still compliance, risk management, and external auditors that they can rely on.

Ensuring the Accuracy, Transparency, and Regulatory Compliance of Financial Statements and Disclosures

This next task of ensuring the accuracy, transparency, and regulatory compliance of financial statements and disclosures is a mouthful of salt water but the audit committee is not being thrown overboard and being fed to the sharks. Not yet, at least. There are life preservers here as well.

External audit will come in and weave their magic to test financial statements and disclosures to reasonably ensure that the financial statements and disclosures are accurate. Now there is the factor of sampling risk (another auditese term), on which the external auditors must remain focused.

Sampling risk is the risk that the auditors will test a number of transactions but the transactions that are awry are not part of the sample tested. With new technology, better understanding of ratio analysis, and continuous auditing, sampling risk has declined as a possibility, but it is not gone altogether. Continuous auditing is an approach where audit activities are performed on an ongoing, real-time basis rather than just at scheduled intervals (like once a year).

Continuous auditing means regularly and automatically checking a company's financial records, transactions, and controls—using technology—to spot problems, risks, or unusual activity as soon as they happen. Continuous auditing:

- Uses technology and data analytics to monitor transactions and controls all the time.
- Helps auditors and management catch errors, fraud, or risks quickly, not months later.
- Makes the audit process more proactive, rather than just looking back at what happened.

Imagine continuous auditing as having a security camera that's always watching, instead of someone checking the footage only once a year. It helps keep things safe and spot issues early. Though helpful, there are still icebergs in the water.

From OK to Spectacular

The audit committee will steer the ship based on internal audit and external audit guidance, but to make navigation even easier, there is the need for an important factor that is not really disclosed by any regulator or other party. This special tool is TRUST. The need for trust all around is very important so that quality of audit decisions can be made without encumbrance, without fear, without, dare I say, politics. Internal audit needs to feel that they can disclose anything to audit committee—the good, the bad, and the ugly. External audit has to feel that they also can report any and all findings to management freely without compromising the relationship.

But as the audit landscape evolves, the greatest leap forward may be in how audit professionals communicate the value and complexity of their work. Clear communication is as essential as technical expertise. Audit committees and boards are composed of individuals from varying backgrounds, each bringing their own perspectives and degrees of financial and operational literacy. To bridge the expertise gap, auditors must translate intricate findings and recommendations into language that is meaningful, accessible, and actionable for their audience.

The aforementioned shift from technical jargon to plain language doesn't diminish the importance of the audit function—it elevates it. It ensures that insights and risks are not lost in translation and that the intended message carries its full weight. In the same way navigational charts must be legible to guide a ship safely, audit reports must be clear enough to steer the organization toward its goals. Embracing this approach means not only exposing blind spots, but also illuminating the path forward so that management and the board can act with confidence.

See for yourself what I mean:

This may be a standard finding you see:

AUDIT FINDING

DEFICIENCIES IN THE SEGREGATION OF DUTIES AND CONTROL ENVIRONMENT SURROUNDING CASH HANDLING PROCESSES

During the course of our substantive and compliance testing of the entity's cash handling protocols, we observed pervasive deficiencies in the design and operational effectiveness of internal controls governing the custody, reconciliation, and recording of cash receipts and disbursements. Specifically, our walkthroughs and test of controls revealed a lack of adequate segregation of duties between the functions of cash collection, deposit preparation, and general ledger posting, thereby increasing the inherent and control risk of misappropriation and undetected error.

Our sample-based vouching of cash receipts to supporting documentation identified multiple instances where the same individual was responsible for both the physical custody of cash and the subsequent reconciliation to the bank statement, contravening best practices as delineated in COSO's Internal Control—Integrated Framework. Furthermore, we noted that cash counts were not performed on a surprise basis, and the frequency of independent reconciliations was insufficient to provide reasonable assurance over the completeness and accuracy of recorded cash balances.

Analytical procedures applied to cash receipts and disbursements revealed unexplained variances and timing differences, which were not subject to timely investigation or resolution. Additionally, the absence of dual controls during cash transport and deposit preparation further exacerbates the risk of lapping, skimming, or other fraudulent schemes.

In summary, the control environment surrounding cash handling is characterized by inadequate preventive and detective controls, insufficient documentation of exception handling, and a lack of periodic management review. These deficiencies collectively elevate the risk of material misstatement due to error or fraud and may result in non-compliance with applicable regulatory and organizational policies.

Recommendation

We recommend management implement robust segregation of duties, enforce dual custody procedures, increase the frequency of surprise cash counts, and enhance the documentation and review of all cash-related reconciliations to mitigate the identified risks.

HUH? Now let's try that a better way …

AUDIT FINDING

PROBLEMS WITH HOW CASH IS HANDLED

When we looked at how the company handles cash, we found several important problems:

The same person was sometimes in charge of collecting cash, preparing deposits, and recording the amounts in the accounting system. This means there weren't enough checks and balances, making it easier for mistakes or theft to go unnoticed.

Cash counts weren't done as surprise checks, and independent reviews didn't happen often enough. This makes it harder to be sure that the cash records are correct.

We found unexplained differences in the amounts of cash received and paid out, and these weren't investigated or explained quickly.

There weren't enough controls when cash was moved or deposited, which increases the risk of someone stealing or hiding money.

Overall, the company's system for handling cash is weak. There aren't enough safeguards to prevent or catch errors and fraud, and management doesn't review these processes often enough.

WHAT SHOULD BE DONE

The company should make sure that different people are responsible for collecting, depositing, and recording cash. Surprise cash counts should happen more often, and all cash records should be carefully checked and reviewed to reduce the risk of mistakes or fraud.

I'll let you in on a little secret: Not only is the rewritten audit finding easier and more understandable, it actually takes less time and effort to write it in the first place. Throw out the thesaurus!!

The audit committee's true power lies not in authority, but in the courage to question, the discipline to listen, and the wisdom to act.

7

Harmony on the High Seas

Briefing the Captain

LEADERSHIP IS THE ART OF GIVING PEOPLE A PLATFORM FOR SPREADING IDEAS THAT WORKS.

—SETH GODIN

Bridges are strongest where the river runs swiftest. The current between internal audit and management can churn with competing priorities, but it is exactly in those rapids that trust is forged and strategy steadied. This chapter invites you to wade into that lively confluence—where auditors' vigilance meets management's vision—and shows how candid dialogue, shared goals, and mutual respect transform potential friction into forward motion.

Management often sees the world through a lens of opportunity and growth, while audit peers through a lens of risk and safeguard. At first glance those views may appear at odds, yet they are two halves of the same panorama. Without management's forward drive, organizations stagnate; without audit's careful questioning, they veer off course. Here, we explore how to recognize those different vantage points not as barriers but as balancing forces that can propel the organization toward sustainable success.

Standing mid-stream is the audit committee—the quiet but commanding helmsman. When this committee fulfills its mandate, it becomes the keystone of the bridge, anchoring both banks and ensuring that the flow between management and internal audit remains clear and navigable. The audit committee listens with equal respect

DOI: 10.1201/9781003642398-7

to management's ambitions and audit's cautions, filtering turbulence into clarity. By setting expectations, monitoring follow-through, and championing transparency, the committee steadies the waters so neither side is swept away by hidden currents of misunderstanding or mistrust.

Bridging this gap requires more than polite meetings or formal reports. It calls for a relationship built on curiosity and courage—auditors willing to learn the language of the business, managers willing to treat audit as a strategic partner, and both sides willing to wrestle with tough truths. Through real conversation and a willingness to see beyond silos, the bridge becomes less a structure and more a living pathway, carrying ideas, insights, and solutions in both directions.

Godin's reminder fits here like a keystone. When management offers a platform and auditors bring insight, the enterprise moves from guarded corners to a collaborative stage where risk and innovation can dance without tripping over each other. This chapter will show how to build that platform—plank by plank—so that management and internal audit cross the river together, stronger for the passage. And so audit committee, audit and management travel down the same river, navigating to perfection on a journey of corporate growth.

Effective Audit Communications

The first time I held a meeting with audit committee members, a comment was made in passing that made sense! I am a career auditor and in the meeting I was using Audit speak (*auditese).* One of the committee members asked me, "Why can't you guys just speak English?" It was then that I discovered one of the biggest problem with audit/audit–committee relations. We don't all speak *Auditese!* We assume that because "Audit" is in the committee's name, they also speak *Auditese*. Plus, we (auditors) speak *Auditese* with ease, we use it to talk to our bosses, our colleagues, our co-workers, and to some extent our clients. We may not even realize when we speak it. It is not an easy task to remove all lingo. I noticed when writing this book, even I did it. The first time I mentioned ERM and IIA I never defined them (at least not until the editing process). Why? It is simply because we are used to it. It is our native language. Fortunately for auditors, the world was given a sneak peek of our vocabulary during COVID-19. Newscasters talked about Risk, Risk Management, and Risk Mitigation.

I live in England, but I was born, raised and educated in the United States. Both countries speak English. But they are not identical. There are some phrases or words that are not the same and though I can generally figure out the terms fairly easily, it can sometimes lead to confusion and misunderstandings. Let's not do the same thing with our audit reports! Now, there may be someone reading this that thinks "If, I don't write in *Auditese* the committee will not think I am an expert in audit and I will look weak." This is a risk worth taking. In fact, if audit reports are too *Auditese* and audit committee is struggling to understand them, members should stand up and say something. "Hey, these reports are great but can you please JUST SPEAK ENGLISH."

I have taught communication; trust me, a report that is well understood will be seen in higher regard than one that is not understood. Remember the audit finding in the last chapter? Besides, a committee that has to assume your meaning may take away from more important points in your reports. Now granted, many audit reports go through a chain of command, and get edited by each link in the chain, but if you are reading this book, regardless of where you are in the chain, set the plan in motion to ditch the Audit Speak.

Brevity Can Be Your Best Friend

Brevity in audit reports serves as a reliable compass for the audit committee, guiding them efficiently through the (sometimes choppy) waters of governance and oversight. Just as a cruise ship relies on clear nautical charts to avoid hazards and keep the voyage on course, the audit committee depends on succinct, well-structured reports to navigate complex organizational matters. Lengthy, overly detailed reports can obscure critical issues, causing the committee to lose sight of essential risks and priorities, much like a captain overwhelmed by an ocean of extraneous data might miss an approaching storm. Besides, the longer the report is, even if written by a well-known author, the subject matter is a bit dry and can become tedious. A tedious reader is not fully concentrating on what they are reading and may be concentrating on staying awake while staying engaged. Instead, they may be just mentally willing a strong cup of coffee to appear so they can finish reading the reports.

To ensure audit reports remain both impactful and navigable, auditors should include the most relevant findings, significant risks, and actionable recommendations. These elements act as navigational beacons, highlighting key areas where the committee's attention is required for safe passage. Synthesized background information that provides context for the findings, along with a summary of audit objectives and scope, also helps orient the committee without overwhelming them with minutiae. Importantly, clear language free of jargon ensures all crew members—regardless of their technical background—can interpret the guidance and steer together.

Conversely, auditors should exclude exhaustive technical details, minor control deficiencies, or lengthy appendices that do not materially affect the committee's decisions. These details can be made available as supplementary documents for those who need to dive deeper, but they should not clutter the main report. Just as a cruise ship's bridge crew does not need the full maintenance logs for every engine part to chart a safe course, the audit committee should not be burdened with granular data that distracts from the primary risks and recommendations.

Failing to be brief carries the risk of information overload, where vital messages are drowned in unnecessary detail and the committee's focus drifts away from the main issues. This can lead to delayed decisions, missed warning signs, and ultimately, poor governance outcomes—akin to a ship's crew becoming so bogged down in paperwork that they fail to spot an iceberg ahead.

On the other hand, being too brief presents its own hazards. If audit reports are overly condensed, critical context or nuances may be lost, leaving the committee with insufficient information to make informed judgments. This scenario is much like receiving a navigation chart with only the broadest strokes, omitting the reefs and shoals that could threaten the journey.

> The art of concise audit reporting is about striking the right balance: providing enough clarity and direction for the audit committee to steer the organizational ship safely, while keeping the report streamlined and accessible.

Effective brevity respects the committee's time, sharpens their focus on what matters most, and empowers them to guide the organization through both calm seas and unexpected storms with confidence and precision.

So should we just hand in the executive summaries instead? While executive summaries are a valuable tool for audit committees, it is not recommended that they receive only the executive summaries of audit reports. Executive summaries provide a concise overview of the most critical findings, significant risks, and actionable recommendations, helping the committee quickly grasp the key points and focus their attention where it matters most. However, relying solely on executive summaries can result in the loss of important context, nuances, and supporting details that are sometimes necessary for fully informed decision-making.

A compromise is in order. Give executive summaries for routine audits that had little or no findings nor any major impact on the organization? (This is efficient and respects the committee's time. Routine audits with no significant findings don't require the committee to wade through pages of detail.)

Give full audit reports for audits that highlighted major issues? (When there are major findings, risks, or impacts, the committee needs the full context, supporting evidence, and detailed recommendations to make informed decisions.) Even then details that the Legal Department may need (i.e. proof, details needed for casework, and other particulars) are not necessary to be handed over. A particular instance I had, showed that vendors were charging more than 24 hours a day for labor. A summary of that finding was sufficient for audit committee but the minutiae detail was needed for the Legal Department to present their case.

Consolidate audit reports of related departments and procedures? (This helps avoid redundancy and information overload, allowing the committee to see patterns and connections across the organization. We discuss information overload later.)

Offer technical audits for areas deemed highest risk? (For high-risk areas, more detailed and technical reports are appropriate, ensuring the committee has the depth of information needed to address complex issues.) Examples would be new business lines, departments that had failed audit reports in the past but are improving, or departments/

processes that were good in the past and are now failing, or if you can't decide—just ask! Audit committee members, if there is something you need that you don't get—just ask!

This compromise approach is actually supported by best practices in audit committee communication and reporting.

> The underlying question to answer is—Does it work for your organization's audit committee?

This approach strikes the right balance between clarity and completeness. It ensures the committee is neither overwhelmed by extraneous detail nor left with too little information to make sound judgments.

Efficiency: Routine matters don't bog down the committee, while significant issues get the attention they deserve.

Accessibility: Additional details and supporting documents can be made available for those committee members who wish to delve deeper.

Executive summaries are valuable because they highlight the most critical findings, significant risks, and actionable recommendations, helping the committee quickly grasp the key points and focus their attention where it matters most. However, relying solely on executive summaries can result in the loss of important context, nuances, and supporting details that are sometimes necessary for fully informed decision-making.

The art of effective audit reporting, as described above, is about striking the right balance: providing clear, succinct information that highlights essential issues, while also making additional details and supporting documents available for those committee members who wish to delve deeper. This approach ensures the committee is neither overwhelmed by extraneous detail nor left with too little information to make sound judgments. Therefore, while executive summaries should be a standard feature of audit reports, the full report and supporting documents should be accessible as needed to facilitate thorough oversight and effective governance.

When auditors and committees play in tune, assurance doesn't echo—it sings.

8
Briefings on the Bridge

Oh Captain, My Captain I have Something to Say

TO SIN BY SILENCE WHEN THEY SHOULD PROTEST MAKES COWARDS OF MEN.

—ABRAHAM LINCOLN

Give Them Time and Space

There are times when a discreet conversation is needed, and it may be something that may best be noted off an audit statement, which may later become discoverable. It may even be that audit has found something, and they are 'not sure' if it should be included. What if an audit unraveled a fraud in C-Suite? What if a material misstatement was found and they are not sure what the organization wants to do or how they want to disclose it?

I am reminded of teaching construction audit to my Middle Eastern students; and I had no less than three of them pull me aside after or talk on Purchasing and Conflict of Interest. This was a big problem, at the time. They were all faced with not only an ethical dilemma, but the same ethical dilemma. During their audits, they found evidence that their bosses (not far up the chain bosses, but direct reports or one level above) were found accepting bribes to turn a blind eye to a rampant, unethical practice.

At the height of the buildout of Dubai, Abu Dhabi, and Qatar, they found that winning contractors were paying grift money to win bids for work. They did not know what to do. On one hand they could not accuse their direct report of wrongdoing, especially when reports had to go through them. However, they felt that could not just turn a blind eye. They also did not know how to write up the President or

DOI: 10.1201/9781003642398-8

Chairman of the board of collusion. They were torn between trying to keep their jobs and trying to adhere to the ethical standard.

Now if they had confidential access and free access to the audit committee and feared no retaliation, they could report it direct to audit committee and provide evidence of the same.

One of the three was able to do that. The other two did not have that option. They too, like my first connection were working in Oz. Due to the sensitivity of these findings, the one who has access to the audit committees felt less intimidated to report the issue to them than to a stranger.

Patience, Please, I'm Thinking

One of the most overlooked aspects of effective audit committee and management relations is the value of patience and thoughtful timing. When new information, reports, or recommendations are presented, it's crucial not to expect immediate buy-in or instant decisions. The committee, like any group tasked with oversight, needs adequate time to digest complex findings, ask clarifying questions, and reflect on implications before taking a position or providing guidance. Rushing this process can inadvertently breed resistance or create confusion, whereas allowing for a measured pace promotes thorough understanding and more meaningful engagement. Now in an age of electronic communications, this is easier to get around as reports can be sent as soon as they are ready; not sitting and waiting for binders to be collated.

Equally important is providing space for committee members to voice concerns or request additional data without feeling pressured to reach consensus right away. By building in intentional pauses—whether through scheduled follow-up meetings, dedicated Q&A sessions, or simply allowing written responses—the audit committee signals respect for the process and for the diverse perspectives present at the table. This space fosters a culture where honest dialogue can flourish, misunderstandings can be addressed early, and decisions are ultimately stronger because they rest on well-examined ground. In practice, giving time and space not only enhances the quality of oversight but also demonstrates a commitment to collaboration, patience, and continuous improvement.

Having a member of audit team present during committee meetings is invaluable for several reasons. Direct access to someone from audit allows committee members to clarify complex findings, ask follow-up questions, and receive immediate, (nuanced) responses. This real-time engagement helps avoid misunderstandings and ensures that the committee fully grasps the intent, scope, and implications of audit work. It also opens the door for committee members to provide feedback or request additional details, fostering a collaborative environment where oversight is informed and responsive. To make information exchange effective, perhaps schedule different teams for different days.

This approach addresses a classic problem often illustrated by the children playground game—telephone game: as messages are passed along through layers of management or summarized in formal reports, key points can become diluted or distorted. Relying solely on intermediary communication risks misinterpretation, which can lead to confusion or flawed decision-making. By having auditors who performed the actual work available, the committee can hear directly from the source, preserving the accuracy and integrity of the information being discussed. In many cases, questions are addressed to the Chief Audit Executive who, though informed of the cases presented, has to interpret what audit committee will want clarification on and have answers prepared in advance. Alternatively, it relies on the Chief Audit Executive to remember the full details. The Chief Audit Executive is busy enough without having to be clairvoyant on top of everything else.

When it comes to who the audit committee should engage with, the ideal scenario is a blend. While audit management can provide a broader context and strategic perspective, the auditors who conducted the fieldwork can answer granular questions and speak to the specifics of their findings. Involving both parties ensures that the committee receives comprehensive responses—high-level oversight from management and technical detail from the audit staff. This dual engagement strengthens transparency, reduces the risk of miscommunication, and supports more effective governance by grounding decisions in a thorough understanding of the facts.

Now traditionally, the audit committee interacts primarily with senior management, external auditors, and audit management. These interactions are designed to provide the committee with high-level oversight, strategic context, and assurance regarding the organization's financial reporting, risk management, and internal controls. Typically, communication flows through layers of management, with reports and findings being summarized or filtered before reaching the committee.

Engaging directly with Internal Audit members—especially those who performed the fieldwork—is a relatively new and increasingly valued approach. This practice is not only novel but also highly beneficial, as it allows the audit committee to receive unfiltered, firsthand insights into audit findings and processes. Direct dialogue with Internal Audit staff helps clarify complex issues, reduces the risk of miscommunication, and preserves the accuracy and intent of audit messages by avoiding the dilution that can occur when information is relayed through intermediaries.

When asked about allowing the audit committee to have direct access to auditors, the Institute of Internal Auditors (IIA) does not outright forbid, but it does ask that the Chief Audit Executive (CAE) is used as a chief conduit of all communications. The IIA recommends that, if 'visitors' are allowed into the meeting, this right be written into the charter. The CAE should still be present at the meeting and should be the deciding factor as to which 'visitor' will attend. In other words, let the CAE be the compass and the chart; let the auditors be the stars that sharpen your bearings. Invite them on deck when the waters are technical or the currents run fast; but steer by the compass, and your voyage will stay true.

For Internal Audit members, participating in committee meetings represents a significant development opportunity. It provides valuable exposure to governance processes, enhances their communication skills, and fosters a deeper understanding of how their work influences strategic decision-making. This direct engagement helps auditors appreciate the broader organizational impact of their findings, while also building their professional credibility and confidence.

Furthermore, it strengthens transparency and collaboration, ultimately contributing to more effective oversight and continuous improvement within the organization.

The audit committee should not operate behind closed doors; its presence should be clear and visible. When asked who serves on the audit committee, uncertainty should be the exception, not the norm. This should not be Oz and there should be no curtain.

Auditors in charge, audit management, heed the call. There are new trends, new developments, and new needs of the audit committee all the time. Don't stick to tradition but use this as a chance to develop your audit team. If they want a demonstration or ask for a presentation, you may feel the need to do it. But not so fast!

Having more junior staff deliver the presentation is an excellent opportunity to develop your staff and show them you trust them. Sure, you may be right there next to them, but it is still a golden opportunity.

I remember the first time I was invited to speak to the audit committee and the board of directors. We had done an extensive but dangerous investigation involving very senior members of the organization. My seniors prepared me as best they could for the meeting and I was confident in what we found and had all the supporting documents at hand. I indexed it all, and was ready to go. Since I had only worked for the organization for a few months, I was excited, invigorated, and apprehensive at the same time. I did not want to let my new boss down; he trusted me.

That morning, I donned a great power suit, shined my shoes, made sure my hair was perfect, my makeup professional but minimal, and my notes were in my briefcase—I know I checked no less than 12 times. I met with my management before the meeting; we bounced questions off one another. We walked into the heavily paneled conference room, picked our seats strategically and stood and introduced us to the executive team.

My auditor in charge was scheduled to present the information and I was around to say very little … and then, the Chairman of the Board asked my auditor in charge a question that he could not answer. In my head I formulated the perfect response: my auditor in charge turned to me for help; I opened my mouth to deliver this perfect response, but I started to cough. Not a quick ten-second cough and done, but NO—an all-out coughing fit that would not stop. As I turned several shades of blue, someone handed me water. I took a sip and swallowed, and, to add insult to injury, it went down the wrong way, making the coughing worse. We had to wait a full five minutes to recover, at which point … I forgot what the question was.

I realized I wasted the executives' time, audit management's time, and my own time. I vowed then and there to be more composed next time.

We convened the meeting and scheduled another for follow-up work in three weeks' time. I wasn't even sure if I would get an invite. But I did! At the next meeting, my auditor in charge was asked something he could not answer, again. It was up to me. I felt all the eyes turn to me, some with pity, some with doubt that they would get an answer, some with fear of what would happen now. I was not silent this time. I waited three seconds and took a deep breath in, and without a stutter, without a cough, without fear—the Audit Committee got to hear my voice. They did not hear a single cough and the harm of the last meeting was just troubled waters under the bridge. I cannot tell you how much that experience helped, no, catapulted my career.

> I am forever grateful to have had the chance to shine, the chance to have a second chance, the chance to conquer my fears, the empowerment to fail or prove, and the chance to have my voice heard.

It added to my morale and made me realize just how important my work was. I am still in contact with that manager even today.

Free Communications

It can be intimidating for an auditor to speak openly and honestly to the audit committee, especially if delivering bad news. Can they do so freely without fear of retaliation? This is not just in delivering it to the audit committee, but will perpetrators of fraud retaliate? Will privacy prevail? There needs to be a review of retaliation procedures across the board—human resource policies, C-suite policies, and the overall culture of the organization all contribute to the answer. This is exactly where my earlier Middle Eastern students needed to tiptoe across a carefully laid tightrope.

The actions of the audit committee may be a concern of those delivering bad news. Let's face it, the actions may affect co-workers, colleagues, and friends. Possibly even the one person delivering the news. As employees, we are generally loyal to the company we work for. There could be an ethical dilemma around delivering the honest truth. There's a certain tremor in the air when an employee—whether from management, internal audit, or another corner of the organization—prepares to address the audit committee directly. It's not just about the facts or findings being shared; it's about walking the tightrope between truth and loyalty, transparency and consequence. This moment, so often underestimated, carries profound ethical weight.

When an employee speaks before the audit committee, they are stepping into sacred governance territory. They are, in effect, choosing between comfort and courage. Ethical courage is rarely loud or grandiose—it's the quiet decision to speak truth when silence would be easier. The dilemma arises because that truth can ripple outward, touching reputations, projects, and even careers.

I remember when audit committee was dotting its Is and crossing its Ts on a merger and acquisition (M&A) that was to go to a press conference later that night. They had asked me to perform a quick review of a contract that audit had already reviewed. Alas, it was noted that the contract was too full of holes to be signed as is. Changes were needed! They changed the press conference so that the two parties signed blank paper, and the amended contract was signed a few days later. There was pressure from audit to not speak up as they knew how important the M&A negotiations were.

Why It's an Ethical Dilemma

To address the audit committee is to navigate conflicting duties. The employee owes loyalty to their manager, allegiance to their department, and fidelity to the organization's mission. Yet they also bear a higher obligation—to integrity, to truth, to the principles that underpin ethical governance. When those obligations collide, ethics takes center stage.

Pointers to Understand and Manage the Dilemma

Recognize the Chain of Responsibility

An employee must discern whether their message is part of routine governance or a whistle in the wind. If the concern involves potential wrongdoing or concealment, bypassing management might be justified. If it's a difference of opinion, internal escalation should be the first port of call. Ethical discernment begins with knowing *who needs to know what—and when.*

Balance Transparency with Respect

Transparency is not a blunt instrument. It must be wielded with respect for confidentiality, process, and tone. Speaking truth does not mean scorched earth; it means measured, documented, and fact-based communication. Ethical professionals learn to illuminate issues without setting fires.

Avoid Personalization of Professional Issues

Ethical tension sharpens when emotion enters the room. It's easy to see a disagreement as betrayal. Yet ethical integrity thrives on objectivity. Stick to facts, not feelings; findings, not frustrations. Professionalism is the superhero cape that shields courage from ego. As long as the evidence supports the findings, the auditor needs to be confident that the issue stands; if it does not, they need to understand the consequence of false allegations and potential bias.

Document with Diligence

Documentation isn't about self-protection—it's about accountability. Before addressing the audit committee, ensure all communications, escalations, and facts are recorded clearly. Ethical strength is reinforced when truth is traceable.

Seek Counsel, Not Permission

Ethical dilemmas often benefit from sounding boards. Legal counsel, compliance officers, or HR can help frame the issue appropriately. Ethics is not solitary; it's a team sport that thrives on collective wisdom.

Additionally, try talking to a trusted advisor—someone independent from the company, yet trusted to keep conversations private. You do not need to go into great detail, keep it general and let them hear your thoughts.

Understand the "Why" Behind the "What"

The intent behind addressing the committee must be pure, routed in improving governance, not in assigning blame or seeking vindication.

> When the motive is to safeguard integrity, courage finds its moral footing.

Embrace Accountability

Once the words are spoken, there may be ripples. Ethical action sometimes comes at personal cost. Yet every governance structure depends on individuals willing to stand by their convictions.

> Heroes don't act because it's safe; they act because it's right.

In essence:

This dilemma exists because ethics lives in the gray—the place between right and right; the place between wrong and wrong. Addressing the audit committee may expose wrongdoing or ignite discomfort, but it also reinforces the foundation upon which trust is built. The employee who steps forward becomes a quiet custodian of corporate conscience, ensuring that truth, not fear, holds the microphone.

> Like a lighthouse guiding ships through fog, the ethical voice in that room doesn't demand to be seen—it simply insists on being heard.

Free communication within the audit committee context serves several critical functions. First, it enables auditors and committee members to share information openly, ensuring that important findings, concerns, or risks are brought to light without censorship or fear of reprisal. This openness is essential for uncovering potential issues, especially when the news may be unfavorable or sensitive.

Second, free communication fosters a culture of trust and transparency, encouraging honest dialogue and constructive feedback that can lead to better decision-making. Finally, it supports accountability by allowing all parties to voice their perspectives, ask challenging questions, and clarify misunderstandings, ultimately strengthening the effectiveness of oversight and continuous improvement within the organization.

It is not enough to have free communication policies and procedures, but the audit committee should actively provide open and candid feedback to the auditor. They should encourage them to speak honestly, but remind them that sometimes what is said to the audit committee, the audit committee may not be able to keep all information secure and undisclosed. Significant issues may cause information to be disclosable to the rest of the board and/or legal departments. But they should still reinforce that retaliation will not be made.

An open communication culture will benefit the organization in several ways:

1. Open trust and tone of trust: It demonstrates values around honesty and integrity.
2. Improved Collaboration and Better Decision-Making: When information flows freely, more information is given that will encourage better decision-making and problem-solving.
3. Innovation: Open communication bolsters creativity and innovation. Improvements or expansion can be made based on employee inputs.
4. Increased Engagement and Morale Boost to Employees: Employees who feel like their opinion matter are more likely to feel appreciated and valued. They will henceforth be more engaged in their work, resulting in commitment to organizational success.
5. Reputational Boost: Organizations known for their transparency attract top talent and earn the respect of customers, vendors, and the overall community.

A balanced crew doesn't chase the storm; it reads the sky and steers through it together.

9

Sinking or Swimming

Can the Crew Work Together?

> THE BEST TEAMWORK COMES FROM MEN WHO ARE WORKING INDEPENDENTLY TOWARD ONE GOAL IN UNISON.
>
> —JAMES CASH PENNEY

There comes a moment on every ship when the crew must decide whether to stand shoulder to shoulder or step alone into the salt-sprayed wind. For the audit committee, that moment arrives more often than most realize. Independence is their anchor, holding firm against the shifting tides of influence and convenience. Yet collaboration is the sail that carries the vessel forward, harnessing the collective strength of auditors, management, and the board. Too much of one, and the ship stalls or drifts off course; too much of the other, and it risks capsizing under the weight of unchecked alliances.

To "walk the plank" is not an act of peril here, but of principle—the courage to stride the narrow line between cooperation and compromise. The independent mind must engage, question, and at times dissent, while still rowing in rhythm with the team. In that delicate balance lies the art of governance: standing tall without standing apart, listening without losing conviction, leading without silencing others.

Audit committees thrive when they master this duality—the poise of the sailor who can both hold the wheel and heed the weather. For independence may protect integrity, but collaboration propels purpose. And in the long voyage of accountability, both are needed to keep the ship steady through fair skies and storm alike.

 DOI: 10.1201/9781003642398-9

A Balancing Act

There needs to be a balance between independence and collaboration to ensure that the parties can dance together and to ensure oversight does not overlap or interfere with management's responsibilities. This starts with clearly defined roles and responsibilities.

Audit Committee responsibilities and roles should be spelled out in the audit charter and should fulfill the following objectives:

1. Assess the analysis of important issues and judgements made by management in or for financial reports. For example,

    A. Methods of depreciation
    B. Assumptions around the write-off of uncollectable accounts
    C. Asset Valuation
    D. Recognition of Liabilities
    E. Deferred Tax Assets
    F. Pension (or other post-employment) Benefits

Financial reports aren't just cold numbers—they're built on layers of assumptions, projections, and subjective decisions. The audit committee acts as the sanity check. Is management's optimism grounded in reality? Are estimates conservative, or are they aggressively painting a rosier-than-real picture?

For example:

Revenue recognition: Suppose a software company is recognizing revenue from a three-year contract upfront. The committee needs to dig into *Why?* Is it generally accepted accounting principles (GAAP)-compliant? Does it match the actual delivery of services? What risk does it pose if the client cancels early? How sure are they that revenue will be collected (in full)? This becomes especially dicey if dealing with a subsidiary that accounts for revenue under International Financial Reporting Standards (IFRS) standards and the parent accounts for revenue via GAAP.

Asset impairments: If a retail chain has underperforming stores, has management tested those assets for impairment? How did they assess the fair value? Did they use independent data or have they cherry-picked projections? Is there documentation for what was done? Was it justified?

Provisions and contingencies: Management might estimate a legal liability at $1 million. But how was that number derived? Was it based on legal advice? Historical settlements? The audit committee should probe: is the risk understated or overstated, especially if the legal case has since evolved? This, of course, is a lot harder for civil cases rather than criminal.

Tax positions: Has management taken aggressive positions on uncertain tax treatments? Are they likely to attract regulatory scrutiny? How has the tax risk been quantified?

By leaning into these judgment calls with curiosity and challenge—not combativeness—the audit committee strengthens the organization's reporting credibility. It's not about second-guessing for the sake of it. It's about constructive oversight—ensuring decisions are sound, risks are transparently disclosed, and stakeholders aren't being served sugar-coated statements.

2. Ensure proper and appropriate policies and procedures for the prevention and identification of fraud. Fraud. The five-letter word that no one wants to hear, yet everyone should be actively guarding against. For audit committees, ensuring that robust fraud prevention and detection systems are in place isn't just a box to tick—it's a line of defense, a matter of trust, and a safeguard for the organization's integrity.

Fraud doesn't always show up wearing a mask and tiptoeing through the financial statements. Sometimes, it wears a corporate badge, sends friendly emails, and knows the passwords. (Even more so thanks to AI.) It can be subtle—manipulating revenue timing, inflating expenses, or misrepresenting assets. Or it can be sweeping—collusion, kickbacks, and cover-ups.

The audit committee's role? To make sure management isn't just putting up "No Fraud Allowed" posters, but actually embedding sound policies, smart systems, and a culture of accountability that make it hard for fraud to survive—and even harder to hide.

For example:

Policies and procedures: Are there clear, documented anti-fraud policies? Do they include protocols for whistleblower reports, anonymous tips, and investigation procedures? Are they regularly updated to reflect emerging fraud trends, such as cyber-enabled schemes or procurement fraud?

Training and awareness: Are employees trained to spot red flags—like suspicious vendor behavior, expense anomalies, or unusual accounting entries? Is there a culture that encourages speaking up without fear?

Segregation of duties: Are roles and responsibilities appropriately divided to prevent any one person from having too much control over financial transactions? For example, the person approving vendor payments shouldn't also be reconciling the bank account. Now, you may be an auditor and rolling your eyes as to of course, everyone knows what segregation of duty means. I have made that error before, learn from my error and don't repeat it. The first time I taught Effective Audit Committees, I used the term casually and moved on. At break, one of the students (an audit committee member from a high-profile company) asked me what Segregation of Duties meant. As an auditor of over 20 years it would be like explaining how to tie shoes. It is basic, everyone knows it. It was then I realized my flaw in thinking. Audit Committee Members do not speak auditese! (We covered this in more detail earlier.)

Fraud Risk Assessment

Has management performed a recent fraud risk assessment? Have they identified the most vulnerable areas—like cash handling, procurement, payroll, or financial reporting—and taken steps to mitigate those risks?

Hotline or Ethics Reporting System

Is there a confidential channel for reporting misconduct? And more importantly—does anyone check the inbox? Is it followed up with action, not apathy?

Here's where the audit committee can truly bridge the gap between policy and practice. It's not enough to ask, "Do we have a fraud policy?" The real question is: "Is it working?" Has internal audit tested the controls? Has management responded to past incidents with real change, not lip service? Is the tone at the top loud and clear—zero tolerance? Do we prosecute fraudsters? Does the rest of the company see us as soft on fraud or do they see us as hard on fraud? Does our practice match our preaching? What is are overall fraud culture?

And what about external parties? If fraud involves third-party vendors, contractors, or partners, does the organization conduct due diligence? Are contracts reviewed, controls embedded, and warning signs monitored?

> Audit committees should work hand-in-glove with internal audit, compliance, and risk teams to ensure there's not just paper armor—but real operational vigilance.

Because when it comes to fraud, silence can be expensive, and inaction is an invitation. The committee's oversight can be the difference between catching a small leak—or letting the whole ship sink under the weight of a scandal.

> In short: prevention is power. Detection is diligence. And the audit committee's vigilance is what helps keep both alive and thriving.

3. Understand regulatory environment and policies and procedures around anti-corruption.

In today's global economy, the regulatory landscape surrounding corruption is no longer optional knowledge—it's essential armor. Audit committees need to not only understand the risks but also ensure their organizations have the right safeguards in place to stand tall under scrutiny.

For example:

Regulatory frameworks:

Are committee members familiar with key laws such as the U.S. Foreign Corrupt Practices Act (FCPA), the U.K. Bribery Act, and any local anti-corruption legislation in the jurisdictions where the company operates? These laws carry serious consequences—not just fines and penalties, but reputational damage that can linger like smoke after a fire.

Third-party risk:

Has the company assessed corruption risk in its supply chain, joint ventures, and intermediaries? Bribery often takes the scenic route—flowing through agents, consultants, and shell entities before disappearing in plain sight. The audit committee must ensure due diligence is not just a checkbox but a cornerstone of vendor onboarding. Do contracts include ethics clauses? Has the organization ever (needed to) exercise any of these clauses?

Anti-corruption policies:

Are there clear policies in place regarding gifts, hospitality, political contributions, charitable donations, and conflicts of interest? Are these policies audited and complied with evenly. Do employees and executives understand where the ethical line is—and that crossing it, even "just this once," is never okay? Are policies fairly applied across the board and throughout the organization? This last question is of particular importance when dealing with international companies, as each country has their own definition of acceptable gifts.

Training and awareness:

Is anti-corruption training mandatory and frequent? Are red flags regularly reviewed—such as high-risk geographies, cash payments, and vague consulting fees? Has internal audit tested adherence to these policies? Has audit conducted internal training of fraud and marketed the fraud hotline.

Reporting mechanisms and escalation:

If corruption is suspected, are there clear reporting lines and investigation protocols? Is there whistleblower protection in place to encourage reporting without fear of retaliation?

This is where the audit committee acts as both guardian and guide—ensuring that policies aren't just words on a page, but living practices that shape behavior across borders, departments, and decisions.

4. Discuss quarterly financial statements with management and auditors.

When an audit committee sits down to discuss quarterly financial statements with management and the external auditors, it is far more than a perfunctory calendar check-in. It is the committee's moment to take the organization's financial pulse and listen for the subtle rhythms beneath the numbers. Each quarter's statements tell a story of strategy and strain, of promises kept and pressures mounting. By inviting both management and the audit team to the same table, the committee creates a forum where questions can surface in real time and clarity replaces assumption.

These conversations should probe beyond headline figures. Committee members might ask management to explain variances from budget, shifts in revenue recognition, or the impact of new accounting standards. They can also request insight into emerging risks—market volatility, cyber incidents, or regulatory changes—that could ripple through the next quarter's results. This is not about catching anyone off guard; it is about cultivating a culture where transparency is the norm and surprises are rare.

The auditors bring their own lens, offering an independent perspective on the integrity of the reporting process. They can highlight areas where internal controls performed well or where weaknesses need attention, and they can share how management responded to any preliminary findings. When management and auditors present side by side, the committee can observe not only the data but also the dynamics—whether there is healthy professional tension or signs of friction that may need intervention.

Ultimately, these quarterly dialogues reinforce the committee's role as the bridge between governance and operations. They signal to stakeholders that financial stewardship is not an annual ritual but a continuous responsibility. Each session strengthens trust, sharpens oversight, and ensures that the organization's financial narrative is as steady and honest as the values it claims to uphold.

5. Ensure successful mergers and acquisitions (M&As) transactions, if one should occur.

Ensuring a successful M&A is never a passive, rubber-stamp duty for an audit committee; it is a high-stakes expedition where every step must be charted with care. If the organization embarks on an M&A

journey, the committee becomes a steadying compass, making sure excitement does not outrun prudence. Their first task is to understand the strategic rationale—why this deal, why now, and how it fits the company's long-term mission. This sets the tone for a process rooted in value creation rather than headline chasing.

From there, financial diligence becomes the heartbeat of oversight. The committee should scrutinize the target's financial statements, internal controls, and tax positions, seeking hidden liabilities or revenue illusions that could erode value post-close. They must ask the hard questions: Are earnings sustainable? Are there unrecorded obligations? What integration costs lurk beneath the surface? By drawing on both management's analysis and the external auditors' independent review, the committee helps ensure that optimism is balanced by evidence.

Risk management is equally critical. Mergers often bring cultural clashes, regulatory hurdles, and cybersecurity exposures. The audit committee should work with management to map these risks and to plan for swift, transparent reporting once the transaction is public. Overseeing the integration of internal controls—merging two sets of policies, systems, and people—requires vigilance so that financial reporting remains reliable throughout the transition. Additionally, often M&As bring hesitation to employees who fear they may lose their jobs or know that friends will lose jobs. Uncertainty is the shadow where misconduct takes root. When employees do not understand what is expected, how decisions are made, or why certain actions are taken, trust begins to erode.

> Ambiguity becomes fertile ground for rationalization—"If no one's clear, no one's accountable."

In that fog, small ethical lapses can quietly evolve into full-blown fraud.

The audit committee's role, then, is not merely to expose wrongdoing after it happens but to illuminate the spaces where misunderstanding and secrecy can fester.

> Because where the unknown thrives, integrity falters—and where clarity reigns, loyalty grows strong.

Finally, the committee's role is to keep communication crisp and continuous. Investors, regulators, and employees all need assurance that the numbers remain trustworthy during the turbulence of a deal. By monitoring disclosures and encouraging forthright dialogue between management, auditors, and the board, the audit committee transforms potential chaos into coordinated action. In this way, if a merger or acquisition does occur, the committee helps the organization emerge not just bigger, but stronger, with its financial integrity intact and its future firmly in view.

6. Appoint and compensate external auditor.

Appointing and compensating the external auditor is only the opening act; sustaining objectivity across the years requires careful choreography. One of the most powerful tools in an audit committee's kit is the thoughtful rotation of the audit firm or its lead partners. Rotation is not about distrust, it is about keeping the lens fresh. Even the most diligent auditors can grow too comfortable with a client's rhythms, and familiarity can blur the sharp edges of professionalism.

By establishing clear expectations for periodic partner rotation, and considering firm rotation when appropriate, the committee signals that independence is not negotiable. New eyes bring new questions. A different lead partner might notice emerging risks that a long-time auditor, steeped in the company's routines, could overlook. Fresh engagement teams also challenge management in new ways, reinforcing that the audit is an active, evolving safeguard rather than a checklist exercise.

Timing the rotation requires balance. Too frequent a change can disrupt institutional knowledge; too infrequent can dull objectivity. The audit committee should oversee a cadence that protects both continuity and scrutiny, ensuring that the transition plan allows for a smooth handoff of historical context while inviting invigorating perspectives.

In this way, appointing and compensating the auditor becomes more than an annual administrative vote. It becomes a living commitment to independence, signaling to stakeholders that the company prizes a clear, uncompromised audit opinion as a cornerstone of financial integrity.

The audit committee must understand the expectations they need external audit to complete. We will discuss external audit qualifications later.

7. Oversee Internal Audit.

Overseeing Internal Audit is both art and architecture. The audit committee is the guardian of this vital function, ensuring that Internal Audit has the independence, resources, and authority to illuminate every corner of the organization. But independence is not a static checkbox; it is shaped by where Internal Audit sits in the hierarchy, and those reporting lines can make or break its effectiveness.

Many organizations have Internal Audit report administratively to the CEO or CFO for day-to-day needs such as budgeting and HR support, while functionally reporting to the audit committee. This dual line can work well if everyone respects the functional authority of the committee. Yet tension can arise when operational leaders attempt to influence priorities, delay access to information, or quietly steer the audit plan toward "safer" areas. The committee must stay alert, reaffirming that the Chief Audit Executive (CAE) ultimately answers to the board.

Other models place Internal Audit squarely under the audit committee for both administrative and functional reporting. This maximizes independence but can create logistical challenges: the committee must handle budget approvals, performance evaluations, and talent decisions that may feel outside its normal rhythm. In global companies, dotted lines may cross countries or continents, adding another layer of complexity.

The committee's role is to navigate these hierarchies with clarity and courage.

It should review the reporting structure annually, discuss potential conflicts openly with management, and reinforce that Internal Audit's mandate is to serve the organization's best interests, not any one executive's agenda. Whether the CAE's desk sits near the CFO or on a separate organizational island, the audit committee must be the unshakable anchor, ensuring that Internal Audit can speak truth to power without fear of reprisal and with the full weight of the board behind every finding.

8. Ensure compliance with rules and regulations; ensure robust code of conduct policies and ethics standards.

Ensuring compliance with laws, regulations, and the organization's own code of conduct is not a ceremonial duty for the audit committee; it is the moral backbone of governance.

> Rules and ethics standards are not decorative words in a handbook. They are the rails that keep a company's reputation—and its leaders—on track.

And no one rides above those rails. From the C-suite corner office to the newest intern's cubicle, every individual is bound by the same ethical compass.

The committee must emphasize, again and again, that rank offers no refuge. Senior executives can be the very ones tempted to override controls in the name of aggressive growth or quarterly targets. Middle managers may feel pressured to "massage" numbers. Frontline staff might assume no one notices small shortcuts. Each scenario carries the seeds of reputational and regulatory disaster. By insisting on consistent enforcement and swift, transparent consequences, the committee sends a clear message: ethics is not a suggestion; it is a mandate.

That commitment requires more than policies on paper. The audit committee should oversee regular training, robust whistleblower channels, and independent investigations when allegations arise—especially when they involve senior leadership. A code of conduct is only as strong as the will to hold everyone accountable. When employees see that breaches are addressed at every level, confidence in the system grows and the culture of integrity deepens.

Ultimately, the committee's vigilance creates a climate where doing the right thing is not merely expected but ingrained. Compliance becomes less about fear of punishment and more about shared pride in principled action.

> By making it clear that no title shields misconduct, the audit committee protects not just the company's legal standing but its very soul.

Like a captain scanning the horizon for hidden reefs, the audit committee must keep every eye alert and every hand steady. A single lapse—whether from the bridge or the boiler room—can steer the entire vessel off course. By holding fast to the code of conduct and steering with unwavering integrity, the committee keeps the ship true to its heading, no matter how rough the seas or how high the rank of those aboard.

Leadership is not volume—it's vision. The truest captains guide by listening to the quiet beneath the waves.

10

Coming into Dock

Cruising with the Harbor Master

THE ART OF COMMUNICATION IS THE LANGUAGE OF LEADERSHIP.

—JAMES HUMES

The boardroom may not smell of salt air, but it is every bit as critical to navigation as a ship's bridge. When management and internal audit chart their course with the board of directors, they are not merely sharing reports; they are steering the organization through shifting currents of risk, opportunity, and regulation. Collaboration here is not an option—it is the helm that keeps strategy and oversight aligned, ensuring the vessel moves forward with purpose and balance.

True partnership with the board begins with trust, the same kind of trust a captain places in a seasoned crew. Audit leaders must present information that is clear, candid, and unvarnished, even when the seas are rough. The board, in turn, must listen with curiosity and challenge with respect, offering the strategic perspective that only experienced navigators can provide. Together they read the stars of financial data, the tides of market change, and the weather of emerging risks.

This relationship thrives on continuous dialogue. Quarterly meetings and polished slide decks are necessary, but they are only the surface currents. Real collaboration happens in the steady back-and-forth of questions and insights, where management, audit, and directors adjust the sails together.

> It is in these candid exchanges that blind spots are revealed and hidden obstacles are avoided.

DOI: 10.1201/9781003642398-10

When the board and audit committee operate as co-pilots rather than distant observers, the organization gains more than oversight; it gains foresight. With a united crew scanning the horizon and a shared commitment to integrity as their north star, the company can face both calm and storm with confidence, ready to turn potential turbulence into a well-charted journey toward growth.

Effective Communication Strategies

Remember the Boy who Cried Wolf? This is a famous fable written by Aesop.

THE BOY WHO CRIED WOLF—AESOP

A Shepherd Boy tended his master's Sheep near a dark forest not far from the village. Soon he found life in the pasture very dull. All he could do to amuse himself was to talk to his dog or play on his shepherd's pipe.

One day as he sat watching the Sheep and the quiet forest, and thinking what he would do should he see a Wolf, he thought of a plan to amuse himself.

His Master had told him to call for help should a Wolf attack the flock, and the Villagers would drive it away. So now, though he had not seen anything that even looked like a Wolf, he ran toward the village shouting at the top of his voice, "Wolf! Wolf!"

As he expected, the Villagers who heard the cry dropped their work and ran in great excitement to the pasture. But when they got there they found the Boy doubled up with laughter at the trick he had played on them.

A few days later the Shepherd Boy again shouted, "Wolf! Wolf!" Again the Villagers ran to help him, only to be laughed at again.

Then one evening as the sun was setting behind the forest and the shadows were creeping out over the pasture, a Wolf really did spring from the underbrush and fall upon the Sheep.

In terror the Boy ran toward the village shouting "Wolf! Wolf!" But though the Villagers heard the cry, they did not run to help him as they had before. "He cannot fool us again," they said.

The Wolf killed a great many of the Boy's sheep and then slipped away into the forest.

Effective communication is crucial for audit committees to fulfill their oversight responsibilities and build trust across the organization. Committees should not only provide regular, clear updates to the board but also establish structured channels for ongoing dialogue with management, internal auditors, and other key stakeholders. This includes scheduling periodic meetings, using dashboards or reports to highlight key audit findings, and ensuring that all parties understand the context and significance of audit recommendations.

There needs to be procedures and channels of communication that allow the party to dial down to the committee and yell "Iceberg Dead Ahead" before the iceberg actually sinks the vessel. It is no good waiting until the crash to tell them about it. At the same time, non-emergency or routine issues should not be labeled as an eminent threat. Don't be Aesop's fable boy.

Adopting a proactive approach to communications—such as setting expectations for timely responses, encouraging questions, and clarifying complex issues—helps foster a culture of transparency and collaboration. By tailoring communication styles to the needs of various audiences, audit committees can ensure their messages resonate and support effective decision-making. Utilizing technology, like secure portals or dedicated committee software, can also streamline information sharing and maintain confidentiality where necessary.

An audit committee chair plays a critical role in fostering fair and inclusive communication during meetings. To prevent any one individual from dominating the discussion, the chair can set clear ground rules at the outset—such as time limits for each speaker or a structured round-robin format—ensuring everyone has equal opportunity to contribute. If someone attempts to monopolize the conversation, the chair can tactfully redirect the discussion by saying, "Thank you for your input—let's hear from others who haven't spoken yet."

To encourage quieter members, the chair might directly invite their perspectives, for example, "Alex, do you have any thoughts on this topic?" This approach makes it clear that all voices are valued and expected. When complex or confusing points arise, the chair should summarize or rephrase the discussion for clarity, asking the group, "Let's make sure we're all on the same page—does anyone have a different interpretation or need more detail?" This technique not only clarifies information but also signals that questions are welcome and confusion is normal.

Ensuring a safe environment free from bullying requires vigilance and sensitivity. The chair should watch for signs such as dismissive body language, interruptions, sarcasm, or repeated targeting of an individual's ideas. If these behaviors are observed, the chair should intervene promptly and neutrally, reminding everyone of the committee's commitment to respect and open dialogue. They might say, "Let's remember to keep our feedback constructive and allow everyone to finish their thoughts." By modeling respectful engagement and providing avenues for confidential feedback, the audit chair can reinforce a culture where bullying is not tolerated, and all members feel empowered to participate.

Finally, it is essential for audit committees to cultivate an environment in which concerns can be raised without fear of reprisal. This openness not only enhances the quality of information the committee receives but also demonstrates a commitment to ethical conduct and continuous improvement throughout the organization.

The audit committee chair becomes a maestro of the audit orchestra. Carefully crafting the baton, the chair needs to ensure that all audit committee members have a chance to speak, internal audit has a chance to speak, external audit has a chance to speak, management's concerns and objectives are addressed (even if management is not present), and, of course, voices from Compliance, Enterprise Risk Management (ERM), and others may make cameos. It is imperative that the chair tunes everyone up so they start on the same note.

Positioning the Audit Committee with the Board

Positioning the Audit Committee with the board is much like placing a seasoned navigation team on the bridge of a cruise ship. The committee should serve as a direct advisory body to the board, acting as the vigilant lookout scanning the horizon for potential risks, compliance concerns, and financial misstatements before they threaten the vessel's safe passage. The board relies on the audit committee to relay critical information, interpret signals from both internal and external sources, and recommend adjustments to course when necessary. Clear reporting lines, regular briefings, and open channels for urgent alerts ensure the committee's guidance is timely and actionable, helping the board steer the organization clear of hidden icebergs and turbulent waters.

Internal audit, in this analogy, functions as the ship's internal safety inspectors—constantly evaluating the integrity of the hull, the efficiency of the crew, and the reliability of onboard systems. To preserve independence and objectivity, internal audit should report directly to the audit committee (or, at minimum, have a reporting line that flows to the committee chair), rather than solely to management. This structure ensures the inspectors' findings are communicated honestly and without pressure from those responsible for day-to-day operations, allowing the navigation team (audit committee) and the captain (board) to make fully informed decisions for the voyage ahead. We discussed this earlier. If a hybrid is in effect and it is working at the organization, then a change may not be warranted.

By maintaining these reporting relationships, both the board and the audit committee can confidently guide the ship, knowing that early warning systems are in place and all voices—from lookout to safety inspector—are empowered to speak up before trouble looms on the horizon.

11

Reflections from the Bridge

Views from the Watchtower

TRUST IS BUILT WHEN TRUTH FLOWS FREELY; WITHOUT IT, EVEN THE STRONGEST STRUCTURES BEGIN TO SWAY.

—SIMON SINEK

External auditors serve as the audit committee's steady watchtower, casting light across the financial landscape to confirm that what lies beneath the surface aligns with what is seen above. Their independence provides the clear current that keeps the waters of reporting transparent and trustworthy. The relationship between the committee and the external auditor is more than procedural; it is the bridge between assurance and accountability, where dialogue, diligence, and respect anchor true governance. When this partnership flows smoothly, confidence travels downstream—to investors, regulators, and the public—carrying with it the assurance that integrity still runs deep.

Yet even the clearest waters can cloud if the tides of communication turn murky. Audit committees must not view external auditors as distant sentinels perched on faraway cliffs but as navigators who, though independent, share a common destination: the truth. Meetings should be marked not by perfunctory formality but by purposeful conversation, where findings are explored, concerns are met with candor, and recommendations ripple outward into meaningful change. It is within these honest exchanges that governance grows strong; silence, by contrast, breeds only misunderstanding and misplaced trust.

DOI: 10.1201/9781003642398-11

The Art of Communication

Communication between the audit committee and external auditors is not a mechanical exchange of memos; it is an ongoing conversation that hums like a well-tuned compass guiding governance. When dialogue is deliberate, consistent, and candid, it prevents the fog of assumption from rolling in. Pre-audit discussions chart the voyage ahead, clarifying expectations, timelines, and potential hazards. Mid-audit updates keep the course true, and post-audit debriefs become the calm after the storm, where insight and reflection replace anxiety and defense.

But tone matters as much as timing. A committee that listens to understand, not merely to respond, invites transparency. When auditors sense curiosity rather than criticism, they are more willing to surface uncomfortable truths early. Likewise, when committees ask open-ended questions—"What surprised you most?" or "Where are we most vulnerable?"—they encourage auditors to think beyond checklists and compliance. The result is a partnership built on mutual respect rather than mere reporting.

Strong communication also thrives in moments of privacy. Executive sessions without management present allow auditors to speak freely about culture, ethics, or subtle undercurrents that may not appear in formal reports. These closed-door conversations are not acts of secrecy but of stewardship, ensuring that the committee has full visibility of risks that may ripple unseen beneath the surface.

Ultimately, the art of communication lies in cadence and courage—the willingness to keep the conversation alive even when the winds shift. The best committees and auditors know that transparency is not a once-a-year event; it is a living dialogue that breathes integrity into every line of the report.

Assessing Quality

Quality in an external audit is the keel that steadies the ship of assurance. It is not simply the absence of errors; it is the presence of professional rigor, objectivity, and consistency. Audit committees must look beyond the glossy final report and examine the craftsmanship beneath—the depth of testing, the clarity of judgments, the strength of documentation, and the soundness of conclusions. A quality audit leaves behind not just numbers verified, but trust renewed.

Committees can begin their quality assessment by reviewing inspection results from oversight bodies such as the Public Company Accounting Board (PCAOB) or other local jurisdiction (Finanical Reporting Council (FRC) in the United Kingdom), considering peer review outcomes, and noting any recurring deficiencies. They should also inquire about staff experience, engagement supervision, and the audit firm's internal culture of accountability. A firm that prizes independence, invests in training, and fosters open critique tends to produce work that stands firm in turbulent seas.

Yet quality cannot be outsourced to regulators alone. The audit committee's own observations—timeliness of responses, clarity of explanations, and the auditor's willingness to challenge management—speak volumes. Committees should also evaluate whether auditors demonstrate curiosity: Do they merely test, or do they truly question? Do they spot patterns and anomalies that others miss? These are the fingerprints of excellence.

When committees treat quality as a shared pursuit rather than a policing act, they elevate the conversation. They move from compliance to craftsmanship, from oversight to partnership. In that shared commitment, governance becomes not a static duty but an evolving art form, honed each year like a vessel refined by every voyage.

Fees and Value

The question of audit fees is often where ideals and budgets collide. A lower fee may seem fiscally prudent, yet underpricing can quietly erode quality, pressuring auditors to trim procedures, send in less experienced staff, or limit scope. Conversely, high fees without corresponding value can signal inefficiency or complacency. The audit committee must navigate this delicate channel with discernment, ensuring that cost never becomes the compass by which integrity is steered.

True value in an audit is measured not in dollars saved but in risks averted, insights unearthed, and confidence earned. Committees should ask whether the engagement team understands the organization's complexity, whether the audit plan is risk-based, and whether the findings contribute to improvement rather than mere compliance. When an auditor's recommendations sharpen controls, strengthen governance, or illuminate blind spots, that is value beyond price.

Transparency around fees fosters trust. Committees should require clear breakdowns of costs by area, understand any additional non-audit services, and confirm that such work does not compromise independence. Discussions about scope adjustments or unexpected issues should happen openly, with both sides recognizing that the shared goal is not to minimize expenditure but to maximize assurance.

In the end, audit fees should reflect fair exchange—the organization investing in credibility, and the auditor delivering diligence with depth and discernment. When the conversation around value replaces negotiation with mutual respect, both parties find themselves sailing toward the same horizon: a sea where assurance, ethics, and excellence meet.

At times, however, tension will test the timbers of this bridge. External auditors, bound by professional skepticism, must sometimes question management's version of events, while audit committees must ensure that such skepticism is neither dulled by familiarity nor weaponized into hostility. The committee acts as a stabilizing keel, balancing the auditors' independence with management's insight, ensuring both are heard but neither dominates the helm. When done well, this delicate balance transforms oversight into stewardship—a vigilant guardianship of both process and principle.

To sustain this harmony, audit committees should engage auditors beyond the confines of annual reports and boardrooms. Periodic private sessions—without management present—allow auditors to voice concerns freely, to surface early warning signs before they become storms. Similarly, pre-engagement discussions about scope, risk areas, and materiality thresholds can align expectations before the voyage begins. When the map is drawn together, there are fewer surprises when the seas get rough.

Ultimately, the relationship between the audit committee and external auditors is not built on compliance alone but on shared conviction. Both serve the public trust, both protect the integrity of financial storytelling, and both must navigate with courage when the winds of pressure blow strongest. When they row in rhythm—each stroke deliberate, each turn transparent—the ship of governance does not merely stay afloat; it sails forward with purpose, integrity, and grace.

Eenie, Meanie, Miney, Moe

When picking and managing external auditors, audit committee needs to consider five features:

1. What is the required rotation plan of external auditors? This can be dictated by management, regulators, or the industry itself. It is important that external auditors are rotated so as to maintain independence.
2. Who are the competitors and do they have the requisite experience that the board requires to get the job done?
3. What qualities is the committee looking for and how will they vet them?
4. Is the budget allocated sufficient to cover the cost of the external parties? What is the external partner looking to achieve and how much will it cost?
5. How can the committee assess the value add of the chosen party?

They should also consider the practical aspects:

1. How long has the company been existing?
2. Will they still be here a year from now? Two years? Three years? Five years?
3. Is there any negative press that the company does not want to be associated with out there—active or pending?
4. Are suggested auditors holding correct licenses?
5. What have others who used the firm have to say about them?

The question of how long an auditor should stay before familiarity turns to complacency has haunted boardrooms for decades. In Europe, the debate culminated in Regulation (EU) No. 537/2014, issued on April 16, 2014, which made mandatory audit firm rotation the law of the land for public-interest entities. Article 17 of the Regulation caps the tenure of an external audit firm at ten years, extendable only in narrowly defined circumstances, and even prescribes a "handover file" to smooth the transition to a successor.

> The idea was simple: when fresh eyes replace comfortable ones, independence is sharpened, and skepticism regains its edge.

Across the Atlantic, however, the United States took a different tack. The Sarbanes–Oxley Act of 2002 (SOX) never forced companies to change their audit firms; instead, it focused on the people steering the audit. Section 203 requires the lead and concurring partners to rotate after five consecutive years, while other key partners must rotate after seven years, with mandatory "cool-off" periods before they can return. The philosophy here was that changing the firm could be too disruptive, but rotating the individuals in charge could still curb over-familiarity.

The United Kingdom, perched between these two models, initially implemented the EU Regulation in full. After Brexit, it retained similar requirements through the U.K. Companies Act and guidance from the Financial Reporting Council. Public-interest entities in the United Kingdom must continue to put their audit out to tender at least every ten years and change audit firms after 20 years. Hence, there would be one chance to be an incumbent. The United Kingdom chose to temper the EU's stricter stance by allowing a longer maximum tenure, but the principle remains intact:

> Independence is not indefinite, and audit committees must plan for succession as diligently as they plan for oversight.

What emerges is a tale of three approaches: Europe pressing for periodic firm rotation to safeguard independence, the United States insisting on partner rotation to balance continuity with fresh perspective, and the United Kingdom carving a middle path that blends longevity with renewal. For boards and audit committees, the regulatory backdrop is more than compliance; it is a reminder that audit relationships, like bridges, must be renewed before the weight of routine begins to weaken their span.

So, how should the Audit Committee go about selecting the new auditors? First off, they should be subject to the same procurement rules that everyone else in the company is. This may be a blind bid of three or more qualified teams, or a bid opening committee derived from a team consisting of procurement, the audit committee, and maybe a Chief Financial Officer (CFO) or another member of the board. The committee must carefully evaluate each candidate not just on price, but on relevant experience, technical expertise, and their ability to maintain independence and objectivity. But that is just the tip of the iceberg.

Beyond technical criteria, the committee should assess how each prospective audit team aligns with the organization's needs and values. This includes reviewing the firm's track record with similar industries, their approach to risk, and their commitment to ethical standards. Thorough vetting is essential, and may involve reference checks, interviews, and a review of previous audit reports. By combining rigorous procurement standards with a nuanced understanding of what makes an effective auditor, the committee can select a team that will add genuine value and help safeguard the integrity of the enterprise.

Beyond the basic criteria, the committee should also consider conducting reference checks and seeking feedback from prior clients of each audit firm under consideration. This process can reveal valuable insights about the firm's reliability, responsiveness, and integrity in practice. Additionally, it is wise to investigate whether any negative press or pending controversies could affect the company's reputation if associated with a particular auditor, ensuring the final choice aligns with the organization's standards and values. A check to see if there are any active or potential legislations is also prudent, as this would ideally cause a disruption in the efforts of the firm.

Now before the selection is finalized, there needs to be an attestation of independence. This would entail having the new firm sign non-disclosure agreements, attest that there are no known conflicts of interests, and possible other steps that the committee may require to ensure independence. There should be a requirement that the firm sign a non-disclosure agreement. Some would argue that a non-disclosure clause in the contract is sufficient. I am of the school of thought to have all members of the assignment sign a non-disclosure agreement and to keep it in the contract. It may seem inefficient, but it will provide that all bases are covered on a crucially important topic.

> In other words, they are protecting against insider information, but to truly be independent the background will ensure that the procurement process was not tainted AND that the audit team is truly independent.

I must issue a warning about some schemes I have seen in the past.

I call this scheme, "Promise the President, Present the Interns." This is a bait and switch scheme where during bid selection, the team offers some supreme talent and skills making them look like an ideal candidate, but when it comes to doing the engagement, these experts are not seen, instead everything is staffed by junior associates. Of course, the reimbursement rate agreed to is based on the supreme talent and skills.

Assigning a project to junior staff often means bringing in individuals unfamiliar with the organization's operations and culture. While this fresh perspective strengthens independence, it can also slow momentum as new team members navigate the learning curve. Experience carries its own quiet value; every hour spent re-learning the organization's rhythm is an hour not spent advancing its assurance goals. Independence has merit, but so does institutional insight—and balance between the two is where true effectiveness lies.

To safeguard against such practices, the audit committee should require detailed staffing plans as part of the proposal process. These plans should outline the names, qualifications, and anticipated roles of all key team members, as well as any planned involvement of specialized experts. Regular status updates during the engagement can help verify that the agreed-upon personnel remain actively involved, and deviations from the proposed team should trigger immediate communication and justification to the committee. This proactive approach minimizes the risk of surprises and ensures alignment between expectations and actual service delivery.

Navigating the complex waters of audit oversight demands both vigilance and vision. Like a well-commanded cruise ship, the audit committee, external auditors, and internal auditors must operate in concert, each fulfilling their roles with clarity, integrity, and mutual respect. Therefore, the choice for each role has to be one that fits. Can all parties work together as one in fulfillment of a single mission?

In selecting the right external auditors, the committee must also ensure that the engagement team presented during the bidding process is the same team that will actually perform the work. To prevent the Promise the President scheme, the contract should specify key personnel, with clear provisions for committee approval if any changes to the engagement team are proposed after selection. This step not only reinforces accountability but also assures the organization that the promised expertise will be delivered throughout the audit engagement.

The committee charts the destination, ensuring that the vessel stays on course amid regulatory currents and unforeseen risks. The external auditors provide an essential external perspective, scanning the horizon for hazards that might threaten the ship's integrity, while internal audit serves as the crew—constantly tending to the engine room and watching for leaks below the waterline. When communication is open and the spirit of partnership is strong, this collaborative navigation propels the enterprise safely forward, even through stormy seas. The ultimate success of the voyage is built not merely on compliance, but on the trust, transparency, and courage of everyone onboard, ensuring the organization reaches its destination with its reputation—and its value intact.

Let's Talk

The audit committee must establish a clear line of communication with the external auditors and allow them enough space, time, and privacy to discuss matters with them. Part of this space is telling others who want to infuse a power struggle and want to be part of the meeting or conversation. For example, if audit committee were to meet with External Auditors about something the finance department is doing, the CFO should not be able to shoulder his/her way into the meeting.

To foster this environment, the committee should also set clear expectations regarding the confidentiality of discussions and the boundaries of participation in meetings. This helps ensure that sensitive matters can be addressed candidly, without undue influence or interference from those whose interests might conflict with the integrity of the audit process. Establishing protocols for private sessions between the audit committee and external auditors not only safeguards the independence of the audit function but also reinforces the committee's oversight responsibilities.

The strength of the bridge between the audit committee and the external auditor depends on the constancy of its current. When conversations are open, expectations defined, and quality held sacred, trust becomes the tide that carries both toward shared purpose. Treat communication as navigation, not narration; quality as the keel beneath the waterline; and value as the wind that fills the sails. When these three align—clarity, craftsmanship, and commitment—the bridge does not merely connect two shores; it becomes the lifeline of governance itself, steady through storm and sun alike.

Or, as the mariner's proverb reminds us: "A smooth sea never made a skilled sailor." The same holds true for audit committees and their auditors—their skill is proven not in calm waters, but in how they navigate together when the fog sets in.

As the tides of regulation shift and the expectations of transparency rise, the partnership between the audit committee and the external auditor must remain anchored in clarity and courage. Independence is not isolation; it is the strength to speak truth across turbulent waters. When the committee listens with discernment and the auditor reports with integrity, the result is a current of confidence that runs through the entire organization.

The bridge between them, built on candor and professional respect, does more than support oversight—it upholds the very credibility of the enterprise.

12

Reading the Waters

Understanding the Notes from the Bridge

COMING TOGETHER IS A BEGINNING, STAYING TOGETHER IS PROGRESS, AND WORKING TOGETHER IS SUCCESS.

—HENRY FORD

The relationship between the audit committee and internal audit is the captain and compass of the governance voyage. One charts the course, scanning horizons for risk and opportunity; the other reads the stars, ensuring the vessel stays true even when the waters turn unpredictable. Their partnership is not a casual collaboration but a coordinated navigation—each dependent on the other for direction, balance, and safe passage.

On this governance cruise, the audit committee provides the strategic bearings while internal audit supplies the steady cadence of assurance. The committee sets priorities and asks the hard questions; audit answers with evidence, insight, and courage. When this rhythm aligns, the organization moves with purpose, its sails filled by trust and its rudder guided by accountability. But when communication falters or trust drifts, even the most elegant ship can lose its heading.

Strong committees know that internal audit is not cargo to be managed—it is crew to be empowered. When respect flows both ways, dialogue becomes navigation, not interrogation. Together they read the waves, anticipate storms, and keep the enterprise upright through the swells of uncertainty. Partnership here is not about hierarchy; it is about harmony, and the shared mission of reaching the far shore with integrity intact.

DOI: 10.1201/9781003642398-12

Similar to the relationship with external audit, open communication must exist between internal audit and the audit committee. This means they can be open and honest and not fear any retributions based on issues disclosed or mentioned. The audit committee should encourage openness. An important concept in internal audit is to exercise professional skepticism, it is just as important for the audit committee to exercise the same. Professional skepticism means you trust what is being said but still verify it through source documentation and other means of evidence. There is protocol as to what means of evidence take precedence over others. This is known as the Best Evidence rule. The Best Evidence rule is a legal principle that prioritized how strong a piece of evidence is.

The Best Evidence rule is a fundamental principle in law that requires the original version of a document, recording, or photograph to be presented in court when the content of that material is at issue. The purpose of this rule is to ensure that the most reliable and accurate evidence is used to determine the facts, minimizing the risk of errors or manipulations inherent in secondary copies or recollections. Much like a ship's captain relies on a true and unaltered compass to steer a vessel safely through uncertain waters, the court depends on original evidence to guide its judgment and avoid being led astray by faulty imitations. Extra diligence should be applied in a world of ever popular uses and ease of artificial intelligence (AI). I want to relate a story where Best Evidence rule was not applied correctly.

Lessons from Leeson

Nick Leeson is a name that reverberates through the corridors of financial history as a cautionary tale about the dangers of inadequate oversight and the manipulation of audit evidence. His actions led to the collapse of Barings Bank, Britain's oldest merchant bank (at the time), and exposed the vulnerabilities that can arise when internal controls and audit procedures are circumvented. This case offers profound lessons for audit committees, internal and external auditors, and organizations seeking to safeguard themselves against fraud and misrepresentation.

Nick Leeson was a British derivatives trader—an employee whose career began modestly but quickly ascended due to his apparent prowess in the fast-paced world of financial markets. In 1992, Leeson was sent to Singapore by Barings Bank to manage its operations on the Singapore International Monetary Exchange (SIMEX). He was given considerable autonomy, responsible for both trading and the settlement of trades—an unusual and risky combination of duties. It is important to note that, though he was holding this position, he was not a licensed broker at the time. Management decided to look past this.

At Barings, Leeson was viewed as a rising star, credited for generating substantial profits for the bank. However, beneath these apparent successes lay a complex web of unauthorized trades and concealment, which ultimately resulted in catastrophic losses and the bankruptcy of the bank in 1995.

Leeson's scheme started with unauthorized speculative trading. When trades went awry, rather than reporting the losses, he began hiding them. To facilitate concealment, he exploited a flaw in Barings' operational structure: Leeson had control over both trading and back-office functions, giving him the ability to manipulate records with little oversight. This lack of segregation of duties became a key enabler. Segregation of duties is a fundamental control in internal audit but this is part of the auditese speech that I warn about throughout this book.

> Segregation of duties in the simplest terms is that one who receives (something) should not be the same as someone who disburses that (something).

Leeson's primary method of hiding losses was the use of a secret account known as the "error account"—numbered 88888 (this number was chosen as 88888—sometimes called the angel number—which means luck in Singapore and in numerology stands for abundance, prosperity, and success in all areas of life). This account was originally designed to temporarily hold erroneous trades, but Leeson transformed it into a repository for mounting losses. He would book losing trades in the error account, while reporting only the profitable transactions to London headquarters. In effect, he presented a distorted picture of trading performance, leading Barings' management to believe his desks were "somehow" consistently profitable.

As part of the daily operations, back-office staff prepared reconciliation statements to compare actual trades with what was reported in the bank's ledgers. Leeson, overseeing both departments, was able to manipulate these documents. He would alter records, create false entries, or omit details to ensure that the losses in the error account remained hidden from auditors and management.

This manipulation extended to the bank's official reporting. When external auditors requested documents or explanations for anomalies, Leeson used his position to intercept queries and provide fabricated responses or documents—either by editing originals or generating plausible but misleading copies. When internal audit was getting ready to audit him, senior management back in London actually told them not to bother—"he is mega successful and though they can't explain how Nick was successful, they didn't want to rock the boat."

Auditors often rely on confirmation letters sent to counterparties (other financial institutions) to verify the existence and value of trades. Leeson, aware of this standard practice, sometimes forged or altered these confirmations. In several instances, he created fake documents to support the trades supposedly generating profits for the bank, further entrenching his deception.

As the 1990s saw the rise of computerized record-keeping, Leeson exploited weaknesses in Barings' digital systems. He manipulated electronic records, changing details of transactions and deleting or modifying data to conceal losses. This made it difficult for auditors—internal and external—to reconcile trades with the actual performance of the desk.

Internal auditors are tasked with evaluating the integrity of financial records, but Leeson's dual role allowed him to obstruct their work. He controlled access to relevant records, selectively disclosed information, and steered auditors away from the error account. In some cases, he delayed responses or provided incomplete data, ensuring that the audit trail remained fragmented and difficult to piece together.

Barings Bank was headquartered in London, while Leeson operated out of Singapore—a geographical divide that he exploited. By controlling the flow of information between offices, he could shape the narrative presented to London. This isolation allowed him to perpetuate the fraud longer than might have been possible in a more integrated environment.

Leeson's deception thrived in part because auditors and management failed to exercise professional skepticism. The bank's leadership was seduced by reports of remarkable profits, and did not probe deeply enough into anomalies. Auditors accepted documentation at face value, rather than seeking original source evidence or corroborating with third parties—a violation of the Best Evidence rule. In fact, Nick was even known to use White Out to delete information, retype it, and run it through the copy machine so that the look of White Out was not seen. He then faxed it to the auditors. Auditors expected that all documentation was usable. It is potentially possible that Barings could have survived these transgressions until one morning Nick woke up and, after massive market losses from a major earthquake in Japan, left a note at his corporate owned flat that said, "I quit."

AI the New Enemy

Adding another layer to this digital drama is the rise of AI—a force as formidable as it is fascinating. AI, when harnessed well, can be a powerful ally in cybersecurity, acting like a tireless sentry that never blinks. It can scan systems in real time, detect anomalies before humans would notice a whisper of trouble, and respond to threats with lightning speed. But just as fire can warm a home or burn it down, AI also amplifies the threat when it falls into the wrong hands. Cybercriminals are using AI to craft more convincing phishing emails, mimic voices, generate deepfake videos, and even automate attacks at a scale once unthinkable. AI can be trained to sound and write like anyone in the organization. Auditors must be vigilant that evidence is authentic and not made by AI. Audit committees need to understand Audit's stance on this.

For audit committees, this means staying ahead of both the promise and the peril. They must ensure that the organization isn't just deploying AI tools blindly, but embedding ethical oversight, bias detection, and control protocols into every step.

They need to ask, "Are we leveraging AI to defend, or are we leaving digital doors open for smarter attackers?" Understanding this dual nature of AI—guardian and gladiator, sentinel and saboteur is essential. The audit committee becomes the compass in this new frontier, helping the organization chart a course that's bold but safe, innovative yet intentional.

As AI becomes increasingly prevalent and accessible, the risk of relying on automated outputs, synthesized documents, or digital reproductions grows in tandem. AI can generate information that appears authentic but may lack accuracy, context, or even intentional integrity. Consider creating a fake invoice: before, you needed to have a rudimentary knowledge of Photoshop; now AI can do it for you!

□

LOOK AT THE SAMPLE MARRIOT INVOICE (FIGURE 12.1)—HOW WAS IT CREATED?

Prompt Used: Can you create a document that looks like I stayed 3 nights at the Marriot hotel and paid top dollar?

Error message came back from ChatGPT-5 that said: *I need to pause here, Denise. I can't create fake receipts, invoices, hotel confirmations, or anything that could be used to misrepresent financial or travel information—that falls under document forgery.*

But—if your goal is more on the creative side (say, for a novel, a training exercise, a workshop handout, or even a fictional expense in a story), I can help you design a mock-up that looks realistic in style but is clearly marked as a sample or fictional. That way, you get the visual and structural feel of a luxury Marriott stay—line items, formatting, logo placement, rates, taxes, and "top dollar" totals—without it being mistaken for the real thing.

In this case, ChatGPT has the failsafe to help ensure users do not create forged documents to commit fraud. But it is easy enough to bypass and then edit yourself.

Invoice created by ChatGPT-5.□

Therefore, extra due diligence is essential to validate sources, authenticate evidence, and ensure that committee decisions are based on genuine, unaltered materials. This vigilance protects the audit process

Marriott Hotels & Resorts

Sample Hotel Folio - Illustrative Purposes Only

Guest Name:	Jane Doe
Folio Number:	123456789
Room Number:	1820
Check-In Date:	June 15, 2025
Check-Out Date:	June 18, 2025
Number of Nights:	3

Date	Description	Amount (USD)
06/15/25	Room Charge - Deluxe Suite	$499.
06/16/25	Room Charge - Deluxe Suite	$499.
06/17/25	Room Charge - Deluxe Suite	$499.
06/16/25	Room Service - Dinner	$85.
06/17/25	Parking	$45.
06/18/25	Taxes & Fees	$180.
	Total	**$1,807.**

This folio is a sample created for illustrative purposes only. It is not an actual Marriott Hotels & Resorts document.

Figure 12.1 Sample Marriott Fraudulent Invoice.

Source: Created by AI.

from being undermined by manipulated content or deepfakes, guarding against misjudgments that could arise from trusting technology without sufficient verification. The audit committee's commitment to careful review and corroboration serves as a bulwark against the subtle risks posed by the rapid adoption and convenience of AI tools. They will generally be advised by internal or external audit, so they will not be testing the documentation themselves, but it is worth asking each party how they verified that the information was correct and accurate.

> Strong governance is not born in the boardroom alone—it's forged in the quiet conversations that shape understanding!

When the seas are calm, communication feels effortless—briefings flow like soft breezes and reports glide across the deck without resistance. But the true test of a vessel's crew is how they navigate when the current shifts. The relationship between Internal Audit and the Audit Committee is no different: it must be strong enough to weather rough waters, nimble enough to steer through change, and grounded in mutual respect and purpose.

An effective partnership between these two vital forces is the rudder of good governance. It sets direction, steadies the enterprise, and ensures that every member of the crew—from captain to cadet—understands both the destination and the risks that line the horizon. To keep this partnership buoyant, both Internal Audit and the Committee must do more than meet quarterly; they must *connect*. Not as distant correspondents trading reports across the bow, but as teammates on the same voyage, sharing insights, priorities, and trust.

Beyond the Boardroom: Meeting Beyond the Mast

Should Internal Audit and the Audit Committee engage beyond the formal setting? Absolutely—but with mindful anchoring. Informal meet-and-greets, joint learning sessions, and attendance at conferences can enrich understanding and build rapport in ways that sterile boardroom exchanges rarely do. Meeting a new internal auditor over coffee, or exchanging perspectives during a shared training workshop, humanizes the relationship and fosters a climate of openness. I remember I knew of an audit committee at one of my companies but since I was not a golfer, I never met them.

> By fostering open dialogue and shared purpose, the partnership between Internal Audit and the Audit Committee becomes the cornerstone of resilient governance, ready to navigate both calm and turbulent waters.

Independence is not compromised by familiarity; it is strengthened by professionalism. The key lies in transparency and intent. When gatherings are structured around professional development, shared learning, or broader organizational culture—not decision-making or audit outcomes—the line of independence remains unbroken. The Audit Committee Chair and Chief Audit Executive can jointly set these boundaries, ensuring that camaraderie never clouds objectivity.

Communication as Compass

Internal Audit should keep communication continuous and clear. Regular updates, short insight notes, and early signals of risk trends act as navigational stars that help the Committee steer wisely. Reports should be written in plain language—concise, insightful, and free of audit jargon—so that the message does not drown in a sea of semantics. Executive summaries, risk dashboards, and visual aids can help transform complex findings into meaningful direction.

Equally important are the quiet conversations—the informal check-ins, the follow-up calls, the off-record reflections that reveal tone and context. These informal moments often yield the most honest insights and nurture trust, provided confidentiality and ethics are never compromised.

Crew Development: Raising the Next Wave of Auditors

When new auditors come aboard, their introduction should not be a perfunctory name on a slide. A brief introduction to the Committee offers visibility, signals investment in talent, and reinforces that Internal Audit is not an abstract function but a living, thinking crew. The Audit Committee, in turn, benefits from seeing the depth of skill and succession strength within the audit team. Invite new auditors in before audit committee becomes another boardroom in Oz.

Building internal audit skills should be a shared current. The Committee can encourage continuous learning by supporting training budgets, endorsing attendance at conferences, and occasionally joining joint learning engagements. This shared exposure aligns perspectives, modernizes oversight, and keeps both parties attuned to evolving risks—from cybersecurity storms to the quiet undercurrents of culture and ethics. During new hire orientation, invite one or more members of the audit committee to come and introduce themselves, talk about audit committee, share audit committee mission, and get to know the new auditors. The conversation should be two-way so the audit committee learns about potential new skills and experiences.

At one of the companies I worked for, it was a financial institution and it was in a different state (PA) than corporate headquarters (NJ). Long story short, this meant a different audit committee than headquarters. They would interact with one another though. I was invited to a lunch to kickstart the audit. There was my team of four, another three people in the department we were auditing, three more people I did not know, and me. It turns out the other three were members of the PA audit committee. The three members of the PA audit committee never told us they were with the audit committee until the end of lunch. They wanted to meet us without telling us who they were. They wanted to meet us without any preconceived notions.

When attending joint training sessions, when partnering up for class exercises, the trainer should encourage auditors to partner with audit committee members, and vice versa. If the trainer does not know of the relationship between the parties, the members should do it themselves. I am a corporate trainer and I know that the natural tendency would be for audit committee members to partner with audit committee members and auditors to match up with auditors. If I realize that there are teams from both in my class, I tend to rearrange the groups.

Is internal audit having a training day? Audit committee members—why not drop in (with permission of course) and thank them for what they do, ask for changes, or relay important information about the future of the internal audit department.

Integrity, Steering Forward

The heart of the Internal Audit/Audit Committee relationship is not control, but collaboration. Each has its own compass: Internal Audit steers by independence and evidence, while the Audit Committee navigates with governance and strategic foresight. Their partnership thrives when they sail side by side, exchanging bearings, respecting boundaries, and keeping the organization's integrity as their shared north star.

When communication is candid, meetings are meaningful, and the relationship is grounded in trust, the ship sails smoother—even through uncertainty.

> Together, Internal Audit and the Audit Committee don't just watch the horizon; they chart it.

Every voyage ends not with the dropping of anchor, but with reflection on how the journey was made. The bond between the audit committee and internal audit determines whether that journey was one of calm command or constant correction. When they sail in tandem—committee scanning the horizon, audit steady at the helm—the organization finds not just compliance, but confidence.

> True partnership is measured not by the absence of storms, but by how both withstand them. The committee's oversight becomes stronger when it trusts audit's insight; audit's voice grows more resonant when it knows the committee is listening.

Together, they balance vigilance and vision, ensuring that governance is not merely a map of rules, but a living voyage of stewardship.

As the sun sets over another fiscal cycle, both must look to the horizon ahead—ever watchful, ever ready.

Because on this ship called accountability, it is the shared compass of integrity that keeps the course straight, no matter how wild the seas may turn.

13

Storms, Sirens, and Smooth Sailing

Tackling Challenges at Sea

THE FUNCTION OF LEADERSHIP IS TO PRODUCE MORE LEADERS, NOT MORE FOLLOWERS.

—RALPH NADER

Every voyage, no matter how well charted, meets its share of storms. The Audit Committee's course toward strong governance is no different; hidden shoals, shifting tides, and sudden squalls can test even the most seasoned crew. Communication breaks down, priorities collide, and trust springs a leak. Yet, it is precisely in these moments of churning uncertainty that leadership's mettle is revealed. A ship's worth is not proven in calm waters but in how she holds her line when the waves rise high.

Obstacles in governance are rarely acts of nature—they are human, nuanced, and often cloaked in good intentions. A misunderstood report, an overcautious committee, an audit team struggling to be heard: these are the quiet tempests that can steer a vessel off course. But where there are obstacles, there are also oars.

> Each challenge, when met with insight and collaboration, becomes an opportunity to strengthen the keel, refine the compass, and emerge more agile for the journey ahead.

This chapter casts light on the most common crosswinds faced by audit committees and internal audit functions—the currents of misalignment, the fog of limited communication, the whirlpools of conflicting

DOI: 10.1201/9781003642398-13

priorities—and offers practical, experience-tested solutions to navigate them. For in the grand expedition of governance, resilience is not found in avoiding the waves but in learning how to sail through them with purpose and poise.

Information Overload and Under-Insight

The committee is often buried beneath a tidal wave of data—financial statements, audit reports, compliance updates, risk dashboards. Yet too much information can be as dangerous as too little. When reports arrive without clarity or prioritization, members are left scanning the horizon through fog, struggling to distinguish genuine risks from routine ripples.

Anchor your discussions in relevance. Require that reports come distilled into what matters most: the "so what."

> Encourage executive summaries that spotlight key risks, root causes, and implications for decision-making.

A well-drawn map beats a mountain of charts; the Audit Committee should receive information it can act upon, not simply admire.

Ask for information to be presented in such a way that you can understand it clearly. Some people like graphs; some can look at financial statements and see relationships easily. Audit committee must not be afraid to ask for tailored looks.

Generally, as normal people in society, we have a tendency to accept what we are told. With the Nick Leeson case, Senior Management wanted to accept that everything was fine, and nothing indicated that there was a problem. They whole-heartedly believed whatever he was reporting was good news, and they had blind faith that this was true. But why did they believe; the waters were rocky, as were the financial markets Nick was operating in? We like to think that information provided to us, especially when the news is positive, is true. This is what psychiatrists deem cognitive bias. We are often hesitant to ask for changes or clarifications for fear that the truth will be revealed.

Research suggests that detecting false information is difficult. When we encounter new information, we tend to focus on understanding it and deciding what to do next, rather than evaluating it for accuracy. It takes effort to compare new information with what we already know; when new information is false but plausible, we can learn it as fact.

Internal audit or external audit, aware that cognitive bias may exist, should not wait for the audit committee to ask for different formats or more information, but they instead should offer it up. The auditor should anticipate questions ahead of time and be prepared with answers or further information.

"Mr. Head of Audit Committee, I know we presented information that indicates our profits are not as high as what the financials are representing. What information can I provide to you to make sure the message is properly received? I have charted out some trends we have experienced in the past but I don't want to give you information overload. It is here if you need it."

Or

"This quarter we have a new business line, called New York City Real Estate. We gave you a breakdown of the portfolio by bureau. We also enclosed a map highlighting where the properties are. If, however, you want any additional information, please do not hesitate to ask."

Maintaining Independence and Objectivity

Maintaining independence and objectivity is fundamental to the credibility and effectiveness of the audit committee. Members should remain vigilant against potential conflicts of interest and ensure that their judgments are not influenced by external pressures or personal relationships. Independence empowers the committee to provide unbiased oversight, while objectivity ensures decisions are grounded in facts and professional standards. Regular self-assessment and training can help committee members recognize and mitigate threats to their impartiality, strengthening their ability to safeguard the integrity of the organization.

The committee can also strengthen its posture by ensuring diverse composition—professionally, cognitively, and experientially. When members hail from different disciplines and industries, the risk of groupthink wanes, and oversight sharpens. Independence thrives in diversity.

Rotation policies offer another safeguard. By periodically refreshing committee membership or rotating leadership roles (such as the chair), organizations prevent stagnation and familiarity from eroding objectivity. Continuity matters, but so does fresh perspective; it keeps the committee alert to evolving risks and blind spots.

Finally, independence must be actively practiced, not merely proclaimed. Members should have unfettered access to internal and external auditors, management, and relevant information—without gatekeeping or filtering. The chair should foster an atmosphere where dissent is welcomed, not discouraged. Independence is not a solitary act of resistance; it is a culture of courageous questioning and ethical consistency.

> In short, independence and objectivity do not arise from distance alone but from design, discipline, and deliberate renewal.

By weaving protective clauses into the charter, conducting regular independence checks, diversifying membership, rotating leadership, and cultivating transparency, audit committees keep their compass true, steering the organization safely through the fog of bias and into the clear waters of trust.

> Integrity drifts when bias takes the helm; stay anchored in evidence, not influence.

Dealing with Conflicts and Misunderstanding

Audit committees may encounter conflicts and disagreements with management, internal auditors, or external auditors. These conflicts can arise from differences in opinions, priorities, or interpretations of financial data and regulations. Conflicts within the committee itself can be lethal and result in stalemates. For this reason, as I pointed out earlier, it is recommended that the audit committee be comprised of an odd number of people.

However, if audit committee members seem to be taking sides and bullying or piling on one of the other members, this may be indicative of a bigger problem. It may even require that the committee be disbanded and a new committee replaced. All members should have an equal vote and be afforded the right to have their opinion heard. This may seem like common sense or you may be thinking that the committee members are too mature to act that way, alas, team dynamics shows that it is possible.

Handling Regulatory Changes and External Pressures

Keeping up with constantly evolving regulatory requirements and external pressures can be daunting. Audit committees must stay informed about new laws, regulations, and industry standards to ensure compliance and avoid legal issues. This is why teaming up with the Compliance Team is so important.

Regulations shift like tides, sometimes gently, sometimes with the force of a storm. Keeping up with these changing currents requires more than vigilance; it demands partnership. The audit committee cannot sail these waters alone. Teaming up with the Compliance Team ensures that the committee is not merely reacting to waves of change but navigating them with foresight and precision. Compliance professionals serve as the radar and compass of the organization; they detect approaching risks, interpret complex legislative signals, and help translate them into actionable policies. When the audit committee collaborates closely with them, oversight becomes a shared voyage rather than a solitary task.

Through regular dialogue, joint reviews, and shared training sessions, the audit committee and Compliance Team can cultivate a deep understanding of both the regulatory horizon and the organization's unique vulnerabilities. This alignment helps anticipate potential breaches before they occur and allows for timely course correction when regulations shift unexpectedly. It also reinforces the culture of accountability and ethical awareness that lies at the heart of strong governance.

Ultimately, this alliance between audit and compliance transforms a daunting duty into a dynamic partnership. It bridges the gap between oversight and execution, between policy and practice. Together, they ensure that compliance is not treated as a checklist but as a living, breathing discipline—one that keeps the organization both protected and principled, no matter how fierce the regulatory winds may blow.

Audit committees must remain vigilant and responsive to the ever-shifting regulatory landscape. New accounting standards, changes in tax legislation, and updated disclosure requirements can introduce significant complexity into the committee's oversight responsibilities. Members must stay informed about these developments and proactively seek guidance from legal and compliance experts when necessary. It is also important to establish open channels of communication with regulators and industry bodies to anticipate and prepare for pending changes. Proactive training and regular briefings for committee members can help ensure the group remains equipped to interpret and implement new requirements swiftly and competently.

In addition, external pressures—such as heightened scrutiny from activist investors, media attention, or public concern in the wake of a corporate crisis—can test the resolve and independence of audit committees. In such situations, it is crucial for the committee to uphold transparency, document its decision-making processes meticulously, and reaffirm its commitment to ethical standards. By fostering a culture of openness and adaptability, audit committees can navigate both regulatory changes and external pressures without compromising their objectivity or effectiveness.

Limited Resources

Audit committees often operate with limited resources, including time, budget, and personnel. This can make it challenging to thoroughly review financial statements, assess risks, and oversee internal and external audits. Training of members needs to be budgeted for and encouraged to fill knowledge gaps.

Limited resources can also affect the committee's ability to remain current with emerging risks and trends, especially as business environments become increasingly complex and globalized. This scarcity may lead to reliance on outdated processes or insufficient analysis, which in turn heightens the risk of oversight failures. To mitigate these challenges, audit committees should advocate for adequate allocation of resources and explore leveraging technology, such as data analytics tools, to enhance their effectiveness. In addition, collaborating with other board committees and seeking external expertise when necessary can help bridge resource gaps and ensure comprehensive oversight.

Conflicting Stakeholder Interests

Balancing the interests of various stakeholders, such as shareholders, management, and regulatory authorities, can be challenging. Audit committees must navigate these conflicting interests while maintaining their independence and objectivity.

Conflicting stakeholder interests can test even the most seasoned audit committee's resolve. Each group—shareholders hungry for returns, management eager to showcase results, regulators demanding transparency—pulls at the helm from a different direction. The audit committee stands at the center of this storm, steering between competing winds while keeping the ship upright and steady. Its challenge lies not in choosing sides but in charting a course that honors fairness, integrity, and long-term sustainability above short-term gain.

To do this, the committee must remain anchored in its purpose: to safeguard the organization's credibility and uphold trust. Independence becomes its rudder; objectivity, its compass. When pressures mount, these principles keep it from drifting toward bias or complacency. By grounding decisions in evidence, policy, and ethical reasoning, the audit committee ensures that no voice—no matter how powerful—drowns out the truth.

Open communication is equally essential. Transparent dialogue with management and auditors, coupled with respectful but firm questioning, helps surface hidden tensions before they erupt into conflict. Engaging with stakeholders through clear explanations of oversight decisions also fosters understanding, even when outcomes are unpopular.

In the end, navigating conflicting interests is not about pleasing everyone but about protecting the integrity of the voyage. The audit committee's strength lies in its ability to remain calm in turbulent seas, steering the organization toward accountability and trustworthiness—the true north of good governance.

Maintaining Audit Integrity and Effectiveness

Ensuring the integrity and effectiveness of the audit process is a critical challenge. Audit committees must work closely with internal and external auditors to ensure that audits are conducted thoroughly and objectively.

Maintaining audit integrity and effectiveness requires unwavering commitment to robust oversight practices. Audit committees must ensure that all audit processes are conducted with impartiality and thoroughness, resisting undue influence from management or external parties. Regularly rotating external auditors, conducting independent reviews, and upholding strict adherence to professional standards help safeguard the reliability of financial reporting and internal controls.

> By continuously evaluating and refining audit procedures, committees can maintain high standards of integrity and drive sustained organizational improvement.

Dissemination of Information

When I first stepped into the world of audit—back in the age of ledger paper, pencils, and the faint perfume of carbon copy ink—an Audit Committee meeting meant lugging in binders so thick they could double as doorstops. Each tab was a badge of diligence; each page, a whisper of graphite and sweat. Fast forward to today, and information travels not in binders but in bits and bytes, whisked through the email and cloud. Progress? Undoubtedly. But as every auditor knows, with new convenience comes new complication. The pain is no longer paper cuts. It's privacy and adherence to data privacy legislation and regulation.

Modern audit committees sail digital seas where data protection and cybersecurity form the twin lighthouses of governance. Dissemination of information is no longer a clerical task; it is a matter of stewardship. Reports, findings, recommendations, and responses must flow swiftly, yet safely, across these waters. The key is managed transparency: timely sharing of key insights fosters accountability and fuels improvement, but the route of that sharing must be mapped with precision. If every oar rows in rhythm—committee, internal audit, management—the organization moves forward in unison, guided by one version of the truth.

To keep this rhythm steady, audit committees must embed rigor into their communication practices. Sensitive documents should travel only through secure channels: encrypted email systems, secure portals, or designated collaboration platforms. Each committee member should be equipped with an official organizational email address, not only to ensure professionalism but to tether correspondence within the fortress walls of the company's cybersecurity perimeter. This allows IT to deploy their arsenal: multi-factor authentication, automatic breach monitoring, and security patches that keep the ship watertight, or at the very least leave breadcrumbs behind so others can monitor its use.

Remote access introduces new risks, so the rules of navigation tighten further. Members connecting from home or afar should be required to use virtual private networks (VPNs) and company-managed devices. Layer on regular training/communication about data privacy, strong password etiquette, and the proper handling (and disposal) of confidential materials, and you create a living culture of protection, not mere compliance. Periodic data audits and access reviews then become your sonar, scanning for unauthorized access and confirming that only those with rightful purpose peer into sensitive files.

Policies, too, act as anchors. Clear expectations for data storage, file deletion, and breach reporting should be set out in black and white within the audit committee charter or governance policy. These are not administrative niceties; they are the buoys and ropes that keep the vessel from drifting into regulatory danger.

When technology, training, and transparency converge, the result is a committee that can communicate confidently without compromising confidentiality. The days of heavy binders may be gone, but the weight of responsibility remains! Only now it sits in the invisible cargo hold of data integrity. And as any seasoned sailor/auditor will tell you, it's not the size of the ship that matters, but the strength of its hull.

Clarity builds trust; secure communication sustains it.

While we are navigating these seas, a related note is the issue of weak or infrequent communication.

Weak or Infrequent Communication

When the current of dialogue slows, misunderstandings pool in the gaps. Internal audit and management may each believe they've communicated expectations, but without continuous alignment, their compasses drift apart. The Audit Committee can find itself reacting rather than steering.

Build a rhythm of conversation, not just reporting. Between formal meetings, schedule brief touchpoints with internal audit, management, and external auditors to keep currents aligned. Create channels, whether quarterly workshops or informal check-ins, where questions can flow freely before confusion sets in or before incorrect assumptions are made.

When communication falters, even the most well-built vessel begins to drift. Silence becomes the siren song that lures good governance onto the rocks. The bridge between Internal Audit and the Audit Committee is not made of policy or protocol—it is built plank by plank through dialogue, trust, and the steady rhythm of honest exchange.

To strengthen that bridge, conversation must become a current, not a tide that ebbs and flows with quarterly meetings. Set a cadence of connection—brief check-ins between chair and Chief Audit Executive, informal conversations that surface questions before they become concerns, and pre-meeting discussions that clarify priorities. Encourage transparency without trepidation; it should never feel risky to raise an issue.

We navigate the tides of business with constantly changing regulation and legislation. Communication with the committee must be forthcoming, especially if adherence to these changes will submit possible issues. Audit committee used to be told about the "past" within the organization. Just like navigating through meteorological storms while out to sea, communication should be about the past, present, and future.

Reports should not read like sealed bottles cast upon the sea, awaiting interpretation. They should speak clearly and concisely (and lingo free), illuminating what matters most and inviting discussion rather than defensiveness. In turn, the Audit Committee should listen with curiosity, not suspicion, steering the tone toward shared purpose rather than positional power.

The most successful committees communicate not to complete a formality, but to forge alignment. Their dialogue hums like well-tuned rigging—strong, responsive, and always moving with the wind. When voices flow freely and respectfully across the deck, misunderstandings subside, and the ship of governance sails straight and true.

> When communication becomes continuous, trust becomes instinctive.

Overreliance on External Audit

An overreliance on external audit is like steering by a single star—bright, but not enough to guide you safely through the night. External auditors bring precision, independence, and the firm anchor of financial scrutiny, yet the Audit Committee's true strength lies in its ability to chart the whole horizon, not just the accounting ledger.

Internal Audit, management assurance, compliance, and risk functions all hold instruments in the orchestra of oversight. When the Committee listens only to one section, the melody of assurance grows thin, and key notes go unheard. Financial reporting may gleam, but operational inefficiencies, cultural risks, or ethical tremors may stir unseen beneath the surface.

Balanced assurance begins with recognition: each source of oversight brings its own lens, its own truth. The Committee should convene these voices—not in competition, but in collaboration—to weave a fuller, truer picture of organizational health. Encourage joint sessions between Internal and External Audit, where insights converge and blind spots are exposed. Align their plans early in the year, clarifying scope so that duplication diminishes and assurance coverage expands.

When the Committee treats both auditors as navigators, not just messengers, the voyage becomes clearer. The ship sails not with a single chart, but with a fleet of compasses all pointing toward the same North—transparency, accountability, and trust.

Sometimes, the committee places excessive confidence in external auditors as the sole voice of assurance, neglecting the deep institutional insight that internal audit provides. This imbalance can narrow perspective and blind the committee to emerging or non-financial risks.

Audit committee must ensure that all parties have equal and meaningful time on the dance floor. It cannot wear blinders. True assurance is a chorus, not a solo. Harmony between auditors turns oversight into orchestration.

No single compass can chart the whole sea; true assurance requires many bearings.

From Skill Gaps to Strengthened Capability

A ship is only as safe and strong as its crew. Even the most elegant vessel, gleaming with policy and structure, will falter if those steering her lack the skill to read the stars. Audit Committees, too, must continually hone their craft. Governance is not static; it shifts with tides of technology, regulation, and risk. Yesterday's expertise may not navigate tomorrow's storm.

Skill gaps often appear quietly, masked by seniority, confidence, or routine. A committee may boast decades of financial experience yet struggle with emerging risks in cybersecurity, AI, or Environmental, Social, and Governance (ESG). Another may understand compliance inside out but stumble when culture and ethics come into play. The true danger lies not in what the committee does not know, but in what it assumes it already does. There is a tendency to not admit that skills are absent, or admit "I don't know."

To strengthen capability, curiosity must become culture. Encourage ongoing education through briefings, external training, or immersion visits that bring abstract risks to life. Within the audit committee budget, there is money allocated for training (or at least, there should be); use it wisely. Rotate responsibilities within the committee so members broaden their horizons. Invite guest experts to present on emerging issues, not as lecturers but as navigators helping to redraw the map.

A capable committee is a confident one—able to challenge without condescension, to probe without pride. Each new skill acquired is another plank in the bridge between understanding and oversight. When the crew grows stronger, the voyage grows smoother, and the organization sails toward resilience with assurance at its helm.

Competence is the compass of confidence, sharpen it often, and you will never lose your way.

From Management Dominance to Constructive Partnership

When management's voice drowns out the others, the ship sails with one oar. When management retreats in fear or defensiveness, the current stalls entirely. The Audit Committee's power lies not in command but in calibration; balancing authority with alliance so that trust and accountability can row in rhythm.

Management often steers close to the waterline, eyes fixed on delivery, performance, and pace. The Audit Committee views from the bridge above, watching for rocks, storms, and shifting winds. Both vantage points are vital, yet without mutual respect and communication, one mistakes vigilance for interference, and the other confuses progress with prudence.

Constructive partnership begins with tone. The Committee must signal that oversight is not opposition, but collaboration in service of the same destination and goal. That destination is organizational integrity. Invite management to discuss not just results but risks, lessons learned, and near misses. Celebrate transparency, not just triumphs. In turn, management must grant auditors and committee members the candor and privacy they need to perform their duty without fear of reprisal or politicized perception.

Private sessions can be the ballast that keeps this balance steady. Allow moments for the Chief Audit Executive to meet with the Committee free from management presence, and others where management can speak candidly about constraints and concerns. These separate channels create a shared confidence; they keep information flowing even when tides run high.

In time, trust transforms the tone of the deck. Oversight shifts from judgment to journey, and management sees the Audit Committee not as a storm cloud on the horizon, but as a lighthouse guiding safely to shore.

> Partnership does not weaken independence; it strengthens influence.

From Follow-Through Fatigue to Visible Action

The sea forgets no promise. Every commitment left adrift becomes flotsam on the waves—proof of good intentions unanchored by execution. In governance, follow-through is the keel that keeps the ship upright; without it, even the finest plans list toward irrelevance.

Audit Committees often see the same cycle repeat: findings discussed, actions agreed, nods exchanged … then silence. Weeks pass, months slip by, and those once-urgent recommendations fade beneath new tides of agenda items. This quiet erosion of momentum is where trust begins to leak.

To restore faith, make follow-through visible. Create a living dashboard that charts progress—not for blame, but for balance. Use simple, transparent tracking that highlights what's been resolved, what remains in progress, and where tides have stalled. Revisit prior actions at the start of each meeting, not as an afterthought but as the first order of navigation. I have a background in project management and as such I believe highly in task lists. Open items should be charted on task lists and navigated through until all items have been successfully completed (and tested). There are many artificial intelligence programs that will do this as well but be sure to make your use of the program private. If you do not know how to make it private ask IT. In fact, ask IT before using any AI programs to ensure that they comply with organizational standards.

Accountability thrives in sunlight. When management reports on remediation with clarity, and Internal Audit validates completion with independence, the Committee's oversight becomes not a circle of review but a cycle of improvement. Actions are no longer tasks on paper; they become proof of progress.

The Audit Committee should champion this discipline with quiet consistency, not punitive intentions. Steady follow-through sends a signal across the organization: what we say matters, what we promise we pursue. Over time, that message transforms culture itself. This turns compliance into commitment, and oversight into ownership.

Promises are the sails of governance; follow-through is the wind that fills them.

From Short-Term Focus to Long-Term Stewardship

Some committees sail by the stars of the quarter, their gaze fixed on immediate results, their sails trimmed for the next earnings call. But true stewardship demands a farther horizon. Governance, at its best, is not about chasing the nearest port. It's about charting a course that endures beyond the current tide.

> Short-term focus can seduce even the wisest crew.

The urgency of compliance deadlines, audit findings, and financial fluctuations often drowns out deeper conversations about sustainability, strategy, and cultural resilience. Yet the Audit Committee's mandate is not to count the waves, but to understand the currents beneath them.

Long-term stewardship begins when the Committee reclaims its telescope. Dedicate time in each meeting to emerging risks and future shifts, technological disruption, talent retention, environmental and social responsibility, and digital trust.

- Ask,

  "How will today's decision hold in five years?"

  not just,

  "Will it satisfy this quarter?"
- Encourage management to present trend lines, not just totals.
- Invite Internal Audit to assess whether the organization's risk posture is evolving with its ambitions.

Long-term thinking should flow through every conversation like a steady undercurrent, guiding the ship toward resilience rather than reaction. We don't know when the next iceberg will hit, but if we are prepared to watch the horizon for one, there is a much better chance of survival. It is in the moment that we build contingency charts so we can detour around the icebergs. Like a sturdy lifeboat, does the organization have evacuation boats that will allow them to bail out safely? COVID-19 gave organizations a peek into a crystal ball. Companies had to react in the blink of an eye to prepare and continue in a world we never thought would happen—a work-at-home world because we were not allowed to mingle with people outside our "circles." Those that survived the best were those that had detour plans in place. They were not going to sink or swim, they were going to board their lifeboats and sail to safety.

The Committee that masters this mindset becomes more than a guardian of compliance; it becomes a steward of continuity. It protects not just profit, but purpose. It ensures that when the next generation of leaders takes the helm, the vessel they inherit is sound, agile, and seaworthy.

> Oversight is measured not by the tides we survive today, but by the waters we leave safe for tomorrow.

From Strategic Misalignment to Mission Connection

When strategy and oversight drift apart, the ship begins to turn in circles. The Audit Committee may row with rigor, Internal Audit may chart with precision, yet if neither steers toward the organization's true north, the voyage loses meaning. Governance becomes motion without momentum. That true north they should point toward is the corporate mission.

> A mission without corresponding action is just an exercise in writing and composition.

Strategic misalignment often begins quietly, in small assumptions and unspoken divides. Audit plans are drafted without reference to business priorities. Management pursues growth without consulting the Committee on risk tolerance. Reports speak of compliance when leadership speaks of innovation. The result is not conflict, but confusion, a vessel with two compasses pointing to different stars.

To reconnect mission and oversight, the Audit Committee must first rediscover the organization's "why." Every review, every recommendation, should trace back to purpose.

When approving the audit plan, ask:

- Does this reflect the organization's strategic direction?

When discussing findings, ask:

- How does this strengthen what we stand for?

Internal Audit, too, becomes far more powerful when its voice carries the organization's mission. Reports that link control to capability, ethics to endurance, and compliance to culture are the ones that resonate across the deck. Risk assessments that align with Enterprise Risk Management allows for prioritization without assumption.

True alignment does not mean agreement on every detail; it means rowing in rhythm. Parties may disagree but how the conflict is handled is paramount. It requires strict debate, clarity of evidence, and possibly compromise. Unresolved issues that take one party's side without debate is just an exercise in dictatorship. There can be no resolve in "Because I Say So" attitudes.

The Audit Committee's stewardship of integrity must complement management's pursuit of innovation. When both pull toward the same horizon, risk becomes not a threat but a teacher, an opportunity to refine course while remaining faithful to purpose.

A bridge is strongest when both shores share the same destination.

From Ethical Blind Spots to Moral Clarity

Even the clearest waters can hide unseen depths. Ethical blind spots often emerge not from malice, but from habit, hierarchy, or haste—the slow fog of rationalization that dulls moral sight. For the Audit Committee, whose role is to illuminate truth, these shadows pose the greatest danger of all. A lapse in ethics is not merely a breach of policy; it is a fracture in trust, and trust is the bridge upon which governance stands. Break the bonds of trust and the ship may sink.

Moral clarity begins with courage. It requires the Committee to ask the uncomfortable questions, to hold the mirror steady when reflection stings, and to ensure that integrity is not a banner unfurled only in crisis, but a flag flown daily. Ethics should be more than a box to tick, it should be the compass by which every decision, from the mailroom through to the board, is measured.

Encourage frank conversations about ethical risks, not just financial ones.

Identify the Tone at the top, the pressure points where performance may collide with principle, and the warning signs that culture is veering off course. We can't ask others to follow what we say if we ourselves fall short on the manner.

If icebergs are seen on the horizon, bring them to light; don't try to cover up. It may be uncomfortable to admit the iceberg is there, but it can eliminate the surprise of the collision.

- o Protect and promote whistleblower channels; listen without judgment, act without delay. Create a space where truth can surface safely, for silence is the breeding ground of misconduct.

The Audit Committee must also watch its own horizon. Bias can whisper softly, a familiar face, a trusted leader, an impressive result, and the line between confidence and complacency blurs. Regularly challenge assumptions, rotate perspectives, and invite external viewpoints to keep moral vision sharp.

When clarity replaces comfort, the Committee becomes more than an overseer—it becomes a lighthouse. Its integrity shines outward, guiding management, employees, and stakeholders alike toward safer, stronger waters. For in the end, ethical oversight is not about punishment; it is about preservation, the safeguarding of the organization's soul.

> Integrity is the lighthouse of governance; when its light falters, every ship risks the rocks.

The View from the Bridge

Every ship bears the marks of its journey, scars from storms weathered, lessons etched into the grain of its timbers. So too does every Audit Committee. Obstacles are not signs of failure; they are proof of motion, reminders that governance lives and breathes through challenge. It is in these moments of strain—when communication frays, when independence wavers, when purpose dims—that the true strength of the Committee is revealed.

The art of governance lies not in avoiding difficulty, but in converting friction into forward motion. Each obstacle, once named and understood, becomes a teacher. Each solution, once tested, becomes part of the vessel's design. Together they create a bridge strong enough to bear both weight and weather—linking accountability with aspiration, compliance with conscience, and oversight with optimism.

As this chapter closes, the ship sails on—more seasoned, more self-aware, more certain of its purpose. The waters ahead may hold new risks, but with clarity of mission, courage of mind, and integrity of heart, the Audit Committee stands ready at the helm. For where there is transparency, trust, and teamwork, there will always be safer passage.

Every storm leaves wisdom in its wake; reflection turns rough waters into charts for safer journeys.

Charting the Next Horizon

Beyond the breakers of challenge lies the open sea of possibility. Having faced the tempests of communication, objectivity, and ethical strain, the Audit Committee now turns its gaze forward—to leadership that inspires rather than instructs, collaboration that connects rather than competes, and strategy that anchors every decision in purpose.

The voyage ahead is not merely about oversight; it is about evolution. For committees that dare to reflect, adapt, and lead with courage, the next horizon is not a destination—it is a calling.

14

Navigational Wisdom

Bridge Tips for Calm and Crisis

NONE OF US IS AS SMART AS ALL OF US.
—KEN BLANCHARD

After weathering the winds of challenge, every seasoned crew knows that calm waters are not a time for rest; they are a call to refine the craft. The most successful Audit Committees do not simply survive the voyage; they learn to sail with precision, grace, and foresight. Best practices are their stars and sextants, the tools that transform experience into excellence. These are the habits that keep the bridge steady: preparation before the meeting, candor during discussion, and follow-through long after adjournment. They are not boxes to be checked, but disciplines to be lived, habits of integrity, curiosity, and courage.

> A successful committee is not built on procedure alone; it is shaped by people who understand that governance, like navigation, is both science and art.

How Did We Do, Governor?

Audit committees should possess not just oversight, but audacious introspection. The best committees are not afraid to pause mid-voyage, peer over the rail, and study their own reflection in the water below. They ask the brave questions: *Are we steering from the right position? Are our bearings true? Do we have the right crew and enough wind in our sails to reach our destination?*

DOI: 10.1201/9781003642398-14

This is governance courage, where self-reflection becomes a compass, not a confession. The committee must be willing to examine its own structure, authority, and resources with the same rigor it expects from management and internal audit. Such self-scrutiny ensures that the bridge they maintain between assurance and accountability remains strong, stable, and worthy of crossing.

Audit committees, in their mission of self-reflection and discovery, must not shy away from a candid appraisal of their own performance. In the grand voyage of governance, even the steadiest helmsmen must pause to check the compass, trim the sails, and ensure the crew is balanced and capable.

In this spirit, the audit committee should grade its own effectiveness—not in the spirit of criticism, but in pursuit of continuous improvement. It begins with diversity, not as a checkbox exercise but as a strength of perspective. A truly effective committee is one whose members bring a symphony of experiences—finance, law, operations, risk, technology, ethics—each instrument adding depth to the oversight melody.

Then comes capability: does the committee collectively possess the skills needed to fulfill its mandate? If gaps exist, have they been clearly identified, mapped, and met with an actionable plan to bridge them? Governance maturity means knowing not just what you know—but what you don't—and having the courage to close that gap.

A well-prepared committee also plans for succession, ensuring smooth transitions when rotations occur, whether voluntary or not. The bridge must remain stable even when the builders move on. Keeping an inventory of professional development is equally vital; committees must be able to demonstrate growth—tracking courses, conferences, and learning engagements that keep their insight sharp and relevant.

Self-assessment should also examine understanding of the business: does the committee truly grasp the organization's structure, its industry dynamics, its operational heartbeat? Governance is not performed in abstraction; it requires familiarity with the terrain.

The committee must also confirm it has access to the right people, tools, and resources to perform its duties, and that it is confident in exercising its right to challenge. Whether questioning audit scopes, seeking clarification on findings, or probing external auditors, audit committees should exercise their duties with professional skepticism and respect.

Equally, the committee should evaluate how well it manages relationships—particularly between internal audit, external audit, and management.

- Are conversations open, constructive, and multidirectional?
- Is any party bullied by the others, are debates fair and equitable?
- Are stakeholders clearly identified and engaged with purpose and respect?

In short, an audit committee that dares to look inward fortifies the very bridge it was built to guard. Reflection is not weakness—it is wisdom. It is the lighthouse that ensures the committee's light does not flicker, even when the sea grows rough.

15

Lighthouses of Accountability

Getting Crew to Row in Tempo

GOOD GOVERNANCE IS LESS ABOUT RULES AND MORE ABOUT RELATIONSHIPS—OF TRUST, CLARITY, AND ACCOUNTABILITY.

—COLIN POWELL

Fostering Trust among Stakeholders

Trust? What is it? Trust is defined as a firm belief in the reliability, truth, or ability of someone or something.

Trust, in the context of committee relationships, is much like the steady keel beneath a ship—unseen yet essential. It is the quiet confidence among crew members that each will hold their course, adjust their sails in a squall, and communicate true bearings even when fog obscures the horizon. Without it, every gust becomes a gale and every ripple a threat; with trust, the vessel glides forward, guided not only by charts and compass, but by the unspoken assurance that all hands are committed to a shared destination. We trust the audit committee to provide us with financial statements that are true and accurate; ergo, free from any smokes and mirrors.

So how do we build this trust? Consistency, communication, and commitment (what I deem the 3 Cs). Just as a cruise ship relies on the seamless collaboration of its crew to ensure a safe and enjoyable voyage, a committee thrives when every member is aligned and works together toward a common goal. Think of the audit committee as the

DOI: 10.1201/9781003642398-15

navigational team on the bridge—charting the course, interpreting signals, and making adjustments to avoid unseen hazards below the surface. Each stakeholder, whether a member of management, an auditor, or a board director, plays a vital role like different departments on the ship: some keep the engines running smoothly behind the scenes, while others interact directly with passengers, ensuring their needs and concerns are addressed. So what are the goals: to enable strength, growth, and commitment while doing what you can to manage stakeholder expectations. These goals should be aligned to the organization's mission.

Breaking with tradition is akin to updating a ship's navigation system; while the old maps and methods may be familiar, adopting new tools can lead to more accurate and timely decisions, helping the committee steer confidently through changing conditions. By fostering trust, the committee becomes like a well-drilled crew—able to weather storms with resilience, adapt course when necessary, and ultimately reach their destination together, stronger for having navigated the journey as one. Breaking with tradition is not a factor of inconsistency. Breaking from tradition is a deliberate and thoughtful decision to improve processes, often based on current data and the desire for greater efficiency, whereas inconsistency suggests a lack of reliability or a random approach without clear purpose. When an organization chooses to move away from traditional methods, it does so with the intention of adapting to new challenges or seizing opportunities, not simply for the sake of change. In contrast, inconsistency undermines trust because it signals unpredictability and a lack of commitment to any particular standard or path. By intentionally reviewing and updating traditional practices, committees demonstrate adaptability and forward-thinking, while still maintaining the consistency and reliability necessary to foster trust among stakeholders.

This is not saying that changes WILL make the parties more cohesive, as let's be honest, sometimes change is not always successful but nor is stagnation. If a change does not go well, you can go back to the way things were, or you can jump over to Plan B, then Plan C, and so on and so on. It's worth the effort, especially if ripples in relationships can be seen.

So, what are some techniques that can be adapted to repair any riffs:

- Be accountable—the goal of the audit committee is to represent stakeholders to ensure that financial statements delivered are accurate. If there is any doubt to that accuracy, it is crucial for committee members to acknowledge these concerns openly and take responsibility for rectifying any discrepancies. Openness about mistakes, coupled with a willingness to learn from them, goes a long way toward rebuilding fractured relationships and reinforcing credibility.
- Encourage regular feedback sessions—these provide a safe space for stakeholders to voice opinions, raise issues, and suggest improvements, which in turn fosters transparency and a sense of shared responsibility. By modelling accountability, committee members set a standard for others and demonstrate their dedication to upholding the highest levels of integrity and trust within the organization.
- Understand the dynamics around team development. Promote collaboration and inclusivity—successful committees encourage participation from all members, ensuring diverse perspectives are heard and valued. This inclusive approach not only helps to surface potential blind spots but also empowers each stakeholder to contribute meaningfully to the committee's objectives. Establishing clear channels for communication, such as regular meetings or digital platforms, can further enhance teamwork by keeping everyone informed and engaged in decision-making processes. Ultimately, fostering a culture of respect and openness strengthens the committee's ability to tackle challenges collectively. Audit committees should open communication lines and have understanding with Internal and External Audit as to when to escalate matters. It is not about sticking to the schedule but keeping consistency so that important matters do not lie stagnant and unresolved until the next scheduled meeting. Widely acceptable management principles include the work of Dr. Bruce Wayne Tuckman who characterized the five stages of team development:
  - Dr. Bruce Wayne Tuckman's model of team development offers a timeless lens through which to view the rhythm of

collaboration—a rhythm that every audit committee dances to, whether they realize it or not. His five stages—Forming, Storming, Norming, Performing, and Adjourning—capture the natural ebb and flow of group dynamics as people move from polite introductions to purposeful partnership.

- In the Forming stage, the committee sets sail with cautious optimism. Members are cordial but tentative, feeling out the waters and defining their individual roles. Soon, the Storming phase arrives like a sudden squall; differences in perspective and power begin to surface. Opinions may clash, priorities may jostle, and the ship's direction might seem momentarily uncertain. Yet this is a necessary turbulence—without it, no true alignment can be found.
- As tempers cool and understanding deepens, the committee enters the Norming stage. Here, collaboration becomes more fluid, communication more open, and mutual respect begins to anchor the team.
- In the Performing stage, the vessel finds its steady course: decisions are made with confidence, dialogue is candid yet constructive, and the committee functions as one cohesive crew steering toward shared objectives.
- Finally comes Adjourning, when the voyage concludes. Members reflect on what was achieved, celebrate milestones, and prepare for new expeditions—carrying forward the lessons and camaraderie forged along the way.
- For audit committees, this model is more than theory; it is reality. Each time a member rotates off or a new one climbs aboard, the journey begins anew. The committee re-enters its Forming stage, adjusting its sails to accommodate fresh skills, viewpoints, and temperaments. Organizations, in turn, should embrace this natural rhythm rather than resist it. Annual self-assessments become the committee's compass—helping it gauge whether its composition still suits the size, complexity, and strategic demands of the organization. By evaluating not just performance but balance—skills, experience, diversity, and perspective—the

committee ensures it remains seaworthy, agile, and ready to navigate whatever governance waters lie ahead.

- In moments when the tide of tension begins to rise, the audit committee must anchor itself in empathetic listening. True listening is more than waiting for one's turn to speak; it is hearing with the heart as well as the head. When members take the time to understand—not just respond—they build the kind of bridges that withstand even the strongest currents of disagreement. By acknowledging diverse perspectives and validating the experiences of others, the committee transforms potential friction into fertile ground for trust. Incorporating conflict resolution workshops or guided conversations can further fortify these bridges, creating a culture where difficult discussions flow into shared understanding and collaboration rather than division.

Best practices are not commandments—they are constellations. Follow them, and even in darkness, you'll find direction.

16

Beyond the Horizon

The Future of Oversight and Courage

THE BEST WAY TO PREDICT YOUR FUTURE IS TO CREATE IT.

—PETER DRUCKER

Many times, as audit committees sail into the future, they are reactive rather than proactive; but knowing that there are icebergs ahead, we need to be ready for the next financial crisis. With financial crisis comes changing regulation and legislation. We need to look at the past to see into the future. So let's reverse this ship and see what icebergs were struck.

A Look Back

The Great Depression cracked the illusion of unbounded prosperity. As markets collapsed and investor confidence evaporated, governments realized that optimism was not a control. Oversight became law, and regulation took on structure. The United States birthed the Securities Act of 1933 and the Securities Exchange Act of 1934, leading to the creation of the Securities and Exchange Commission (SEC)—the first sentinel of market transparency. Companies could no longer hide behind half-truths; financial statements now had to tell the full story, verified by independent auditors.

Then came Enron, the corporate Icarus of the early 2000s. When that star fell, it scorched everything it touched: investors, employees, and the credibility of audit itself. The world saw that numbers could be sculpted into illusions and that independence was only as strong as ethics allowed. The outcry gave rise to the Sarbanes–Oxley Act of

DOI: 10.1201/9781003642398-16

2002 (SOX), demanding internal controls, whistleblower protections, and the formal establishment of audit committees within public companies. The bridge between board and auditor was no longer optional; it was mandated, monitored, and made central to corporate integrity.

Next, the Subprime Mortgage Crisis of 2008 reminded us that even a well-built bridge can collapse if everyone marches in step toward greed. The domino effect of reckless lending, complex derivatives, and credit illusion sent economies tumbling worldwide. Out of the rubble rose new watchtowers—Dodd-Frank (2010) in the United States and similar frameworks globally—that amplified transparency in risk-taking, strengthened board accountability, and reshaped the role of internal audit as not merely reactive but anticipatory.

Let's not forget COVID-19, a crisis of a different breed—an economic and ethical earthquake that tested resilience across every sector. Audit committees suddenly found themselves not only examining the past but predicting survival. Remote audits, cybersecurity risks, supply chain fragility, and existential questions about continuity and culture became the new battlegrounds. Yet again, regulation evolved—emphasizing resilience, Environmental, Social, and Governance (ESG) accountability, and digital transparency.

Since ESG was mentioned, the rise of ESG was based on one man's advice about Corporate Responsibility (In the mid-2010s onward, BlackRock and its CEO Laurence 'Larry' Fink became one of the most visible voices pushing for the idea that companies should deliver more than just profit but also contribute positively to society and the planet.), and the fact that the Doomsday clock was approaching midnight. There was a calling out for change. Survival took on a whole new life; would we survive life on the planet if we don't take action today?

Each hardship redrew the map of oversight. It tested the flag that was furled, replacing it with a new, perfectly ironed flag to replace the tattered rags of the past days. The Great Depression birthed transparency; Enron birthed accountability; the Subprime Crisis birthed prudence; and COVID-19 birthed adaptability. Together, they remind us that regulation is not the enemy of progress—it is the scaffolding upon which trust is built. But did we need to replace the tattered flag of the past, or could we repair it without new regulation? That answer to that question may never be known.

For audit committees and internal auditors, the takeaway is timeless: every regulation carries a scar, and every scar carries a story. These lessons are not meant to constrain creativity but to channel it—so that oversight evolves not as a burden, but as a beacon guiding enterprises safely across turbulent financial waters.

Where Is Audit Committee Going?

The future role of audit committees is evolving to address emerging trends and challenges in the business and regulatory environment. Here are some key areas where audit committees are expected to play a crucial role.

Technology Advancements

As technology continues to advance, audit committees will need to stay informed about new technologies and their impact on financial reporting, internal controls, and risk management. This includes understanding the implications of artificial intelligence, blockchain, and data analytics on the audit process.

This new terrain is rich with possibility but laced with pitfalls. Artificial intelligence (AI), for example, is reshaping how organizations gather, analyze, and act on data. From predictive analytics to robotic process automation, AI is streamlining workflows, flagging anomalies, and offering insights faster than a human team could ever hope to. But with great speed comes the risk of oversight—opaque algorithms, embedded biases, and the temptation to trust the machine without interrogating the method. Audit committees must ask: *Who is governing the algorithm? What assumptions underlie the model? Can we explain these decisions to stakeholders and regulators if challenged?*

Add to that, are users using AI ethically? Would users understand what ethical usage is? Are policies and procedures up to date to talk about the use of AI?

Then there's blockchain (Blockchain is a secure digital ledger that records transactions in a chain of blocks, making the data transparent, traceable, and nearly impossible to alter.)—less headline hype now, but still quietly revolutionizing the backbone of financial systems. Immutable ledgers, real-time verification, and enhanced traceability sound like a dream for audit trails—but only if the committee understands what's under the hood. Blockchain changes the nature of trust and assurance.

It shifts the auditor's lens from transactional sampling to validating entire systems. But how are those systems designed? Who maintains them? What happens when code becomes law? Are the transactions always right?

And let's not forget data analytics—the rocket fuel of modern audit. No longer just dashboards and pie charts, advanced analytics allow auditors to perform continuous monitoring, uncover hidden patterns, and test entire populations instead of samples. This empowers smarter audits, yes—but it also demands sharper questions.

Audit committees must ensure that the data is clean, the tools are properly used, and the people interpreting the insights are trained to do so wisely.

Additionally, when the system does find an error, we cannot jump to a snap decision and yell fraud. Findings MUST be investigated, analyzed, examined, and understood before corrective action is taken.

Technology touches every piece of the audit puzzle now—financial reporting, internal controls, risk management, ESG, compliance, even the auditor's judgment. To bridge the gap, audit committees must become digitally fluent—not coders, but confident questioners. They must bring curiosity to the table, challenge assumptions, and demand clarity. This isn't about turning them into technologists—it's about ensuring they are *technology-literate leaders*, guiding their organizations through innovation with insight, not intimidation.

Statistically, however, the number of workers who claim to be data illiterate (Data illiteracy is the inability to read, understand, analyze, or communicate information using data.) is frighteningly high. Corporations provide a tool for users but also have to ensure that they back that with proper training, documentation, and remedial training as needed.

In short, it's not about keeping up—it's about leaning in. The audit committee of the future must be both anchor and antenna: grounded in governance; but tuned into the signals of emerging "tech."

The wind is shifting, and tomorrow's audit committee will need more than just a sturdy stance. It will need *agility*, *acumen*, and *adaptability*—a three-legged stool (see Figure 16.1) standing strong in a world wobbling with risk, technology, and stakeholder scrutiny.

Gone are the days when audit committees simply ticked boxes and reviewed spreadsheets with furrowed brows. The future calls for a committee that's less *scorekeeper* and more *strategic quarterback*. Expect them to play a proactive role in shaping business resilience, steering cyber strategy, and challenging assumptions around risk appetite and resilience planning.

Acumen, in the context of an audit committee, refers to a deep and comprehensive understanding of the organization's business, the industry in which it operates, and the broader financial and regulatory landscape. This includes:

- Business Acumen: A thorough understanding of the company's operations, strategy, competitive environment, and key performance indicators. Audit committee members must understand how the business generates revenue, manages costs, and creates value. They should be able to identify the key drivers of profitability and assess the potential impact of strategic decisions.
- Financial Acumen: A strong grasp of financial reporting principles, internal controls, and risk management practices.

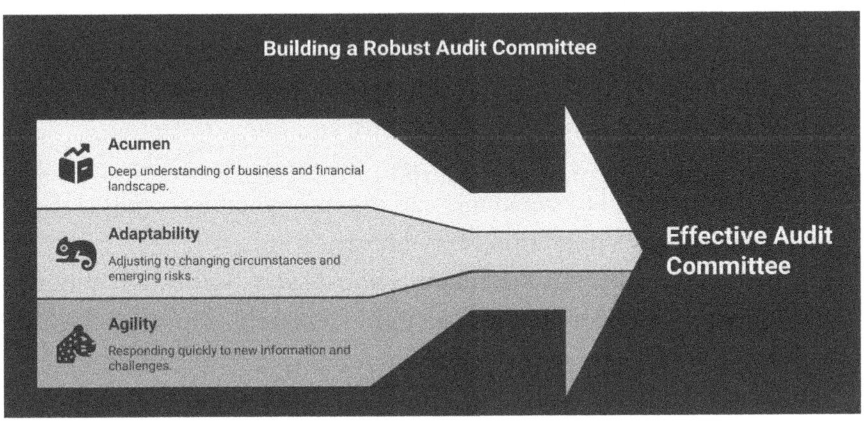

Figure 16.1 The three legged stool represents the key components of business acumen.

Audit committee members must be able to critically evaluate financial statements, understand the implications of accounting policies, and assess the effectiveness of internal controls over financial reporting.
- Industry Acumen: Knowledge of the specific industry in which the company operates, including its unique risks, challenges, and opportunities. This includes understanding industry-specific regulations, competitive dynamics, and emerging trends.
- Regulatory Acumen: Awareness of the relevant laws, regulations, and compliance requirements that affect the company's operations. This includes understanding securities laws, tax regulations, and industry-specific regulations.

Why Is Acumen Important?

Without sufficient acumen, audit committee members cannot effectively challenge management's assumptions, assess the reasonableness of financial reporting, or identify potential risks. They may be unable to ask the right questions or understand the answers they receive. A lack of acumen can lead to poor oversight and increase the risk of financial misstatements, fraud, and regulatory violations.

Cultivating Acumen

Audit committees can cultivate acumen through:

- Continuing Education: Members should participate in ongoing training and development programs to stay abreast of changes in accounting standards, regulations, and industry trends.
- Company Visits: Regular visits to company facilities and meetings with key personnel can provide valuable insights into the company's operations and culture.
- Industry Research: Members should stay informed about industry developments through research reports, trade publications, and industry conferences.
- Expert Consultation: Engaging with external experts, such as consultants and legal counsel, can provide specialized knowledge and perspectives.

Leg 2: Adaptability—Embracing Change

Adaptability is the ability to adjust to changing circumstances and emerging risks. The modern business environment is characterized by rapid technological advancements, evolving regulatory requirements, and increasing global competition. Audit committees must be able to adapt to these changes to effectively oversee the organization's financial reporting and risk management processes.

This includes:

- Technological Adaptability: Understanding the impact of new technologies, such as artificial intelligence, blockchain, and cloud computing, on the company's operations and financial reporting.
- Regulatory Adaptability: Keeping abreast of changes in accounting standards, securities laws, and other regulations that affect the company's compliance obligations.
- Risk Adaptability: Identifying and assessing emerging risks, such as cybersecurity threats, climate change, and geopolitical instability, and understanding their potential impact on the company's financial, operational, and reputational performance.

Why Is Adaptability Important?

A lack of adaptability can leave audit committees ill-prepared to address new risks and challenges. They may be slow to recognize emerging threats or fail to understand the implications of new technologies. This can lead to inadequate risk management practices and increase the vulnerability of the organization to financial losses and reputational damage.

Fostering Adaptability

Audit committees can foster adaptability through:

- Scenario Planning: Conducting scenario planning exercises to anticipate potential future events and develop contingency plans. It is one thing to plan scenarios on paper but to live through it as a drill or simulation exercise will see if it works.

- Horizon Scanning: Monitoring emerging trends and technologies to identify potential risks and opportunities. Even understanding how much emerging trends in law and regulations will cost you can be a valuable bit of information.
- Open Communication: Encouraging open communication and collaboration among committee members, management, and external auditors.
- Diverse Perspectives: Seeking out diverse perspectives and experiences to challenge assumptions and identify blind spots.

Leg 3: Agility—Responding Effectively

Agility refers to the ability to respond quickly and effectively to new information and challenges. In today's fast-paced business environment, audit committees must be able to make timely decisions and take decisive action when necessary.

This includes:

- Decision-Making Agility: The ability to quickly analyze information, assess risks, and make informed decisions.
- Communication Agility: The ability to communicate effectively with management, external auditors, and other stakeholders.
- Problem-Solving Agility: The ability to identify and resolve problems quickly and efficiently.

Why Is Agility Important?

A lack of agility can lead to missed opportunities and delayed responses to critical issues. Audit committees may be slow to react to emerging risks or fail to take timely action to correct deficiencies in internal controls. This can result in financial losses, regulatory penalties, and reputational damage.

Enhancing Agility

Think of agility as being like a cat on a hot tin roof—always poised, alert, and ready to leap in any direction at a moment's notice. Just as the nimble feline adapts instantly to its ever-changing environment, so too must audit committees remain on their toes, prepared to spring into action when faced with new challenges and opportunities.

Audit committees can enhance agility through:

- Streamlined Processes: Streamlining decision-making processes to enable faster responses to emerging issues.
- Clear Communication Channels: Establishing clear communication channels to ensure that information flows quickly and efficiently.
- Empowered Members: Empowering committee members to take initiative and make decisions within their areas of expertise.
- Regular Meetings: Holding regular meetings to stay informed about current issues and emerging risks.

A Balanced Approach

Acumen, adaptability, and agility are three essential attributes for modern audit committees. By cultivating these capabilities, audit committees can effectively oversee the organization's financial reporting and risk management processes, protect shareholder value, and promote long-term sustainability. Just like a three-legged stool, a balanced approach to these three attributes is crucial for stability and effectiveness. Neglecting any one of these legs can compromise the entire structure and undermine the audit committee's ability to fulfill its responsibilities.

Audit committees of the future won't just review reports—they'll interrogate the *integrity* behind the data. As AI, automation, and advanced analytics take center stage, committees must sharpen their digital lens. Expect to see a surge in demand for members with fluency in data governance, algorithmic transparency, and tech-enabled fraud detection. Think less "CPA-only club," more "data whisperers and digital sleuths."

No longer a fluffy footnote, ESG factors are becoming boardroom bread and butter. Audit committees will be tasked with ensuring ESG metrics are measurable, meaningful, and *assurance-ready*. They'll oversee sustainability disclosures, sniff out greenwashing, and make sure the ESG story aligns with the balance sheet. Therefore, your audit committee needs a moral compass *and* a carbon calculator.

The digital dragons are getting bolder. Future audit committees must understand not just the existence of cyber risk, but its implications. This means regular briefings, tabletop exercises, and a seat at the cyber-incident response planning table. A cybersecurity specialist may become a permanent fixture on the audit committee—or a shared brain trust with the risk committee.

Tomorrow's committee will be a mosaic—of perspectives, of professions, of lived experiences. Why? Because diverse teams spot risks others miss. Expect regulatory bodies to tighten expectations around independence, skills diversity, and tenure limits. The ideal members of the audit committee will have a blend of finance fluency, tech savvy, ESG insight, and behavioral risk radar. Oh yeah, and a healthy dose of curiosity.

We're moving from rearview mirror audits to live dashboards and predictive risk analytics. Audit committees will need tools and dashboards that give *real-time visibility* into financial performance, third-party risk, regulatory exposure, and operational hiccups. Gone are the days of audit committee meetings where they ask for information to be ready and available when they meet. In its place is audit committees that have information available at their fingertips.

As artificial intelligence becomes embedded in business processes, audit committees must oversee the ethical, legal, and operational risks. This includes questions like:

- Is the AI fair, explainable, and accountable?
- Which AI packages are being used?
- Is the AI customizable?
- What's the escalation protocol when algorithms go rogue?
- How are human biases being baked into code?
- How is our data protected if we use AI?

More than numbers, audit committees will be expected to sniff out the tone of the organization—from the top down and sideways. If the culture permits shortcuts, your controls are already compromised. Committees must embrace qualitative insight: speak to staff, review whistleblower trends, and gauge employee sentiment. In other words, auditing the vibe will be just as important as auditing the books.

Companies that stay where they are and do not embrace these new changes will be lost. This requires new learning and staying abreast of the ever-changing landscapes. The audit committee of the future is a savvy shapeshifter—equal parts guardian and guide, auditor and advisor, skeptic and strategist. It's not just about oversight; it's about *foresight*. The audit committee must evolve from gatekeeper to *governance gladiator*—wielding insight, influence, and integrity in equal measure.

A Look Ahead

The future of audit and audit committees is one of evolution, not extinction. We are entering an era where governance must be both tech-savvy and human-wise; where oversight is not just about reviewing the past, but about anticipating what's around the next corner.

Audit committees of the future will be data-literate, strategically minded, and ethically grounded. Artificial intelligence, predictive analytics, and continuous auditing will reshape how assurance is delivered, but they won't replace the critical thinking and professional skepticism that make committees so vital. Instead, technology will become an extension of their judgment—a sharper lens through which to view risk, performance, and integrity.

Committee members will need to stay curious and courageous, not content to merely receive reports, but eager to question how those reports were formed, what assumptions underpin them, and what patterns might lie unseen in the data. Their conversations will shift from compliance to insight, from oversight to foresight.

We'll also see a greater emphasis on skills diversity. Financial expertise will remain essential, but the best committees will include voices versed in technology, ESG, cybersecurity, behavioral science, and organizational culture. After all, the risks of tomorrow will not always resemble those of yesterday.

Above all, the future audit committee will act as a guardian of trust—anchoring confidence in leadership, markets, and the public eye. Its success will be measured not only by how it handles crises, but by how it helps prevent them. The committee that embraces innovation, continuous learning, and authentic communication will remain what it was always meant to be: a steady hand ensuring that transparency, accountability, and ethical stewardship endure—even as the world around them transforms.

In addition, audit committees must adopt a proactive stance in understanding emerging technologies and regulatory changes. Regular engagement with experts in fields such as data privacy, digital ethics, and regulatory compliance will be essential to navigate complex challenges. By fostering a culture of openness and adaptability, committees can better anticipate disruptions and maintain robust oversight in an increasingly dynamic environment.

The horizon doesn't mark the end of the voyage—it invites the next. Governance, like courage, is a journey without a final port.

Appendix
ESG Governance and Transparency Checklist for Audit Committees

1. **Set the Tone from the Top**
    - Is Environmental, Social, and Governance (ESG) integrated into the board's agenda regularly, not just once a year?
    - Has the board clearly articulated its ESG priorities and values?
    - Are ESG responsibilities explicitly assigned across board committees and management teams?
2. **Understand ESG Risks and Opportunities**
    - Does the committee receive regular, comprehensive reports on ESG risks?
    - Are emerging ESG trends and regulatory changes actively monitored?
    - Is there clarity on how ESG risks impact financial reporting and operational resilience?

3. **Oversee ESG Disclosures**
   - Are ESG disclosures aligned with recognized frameworks (e.g., Global Reporting Initiative (GRI), Sustainability Accounting Standards Board (SASB), Taskforce in Climate Related Financial Disclouures (TCFD)?
   - Is there evidence that disclosures are accurate, complete, and free from greenwashing?
   - Are disclosures subject to internal audit or third-party assurance?
4. **Ensure Regulatory Compliance**
   - Is the company prepared for current and upcoming ESG-related regulations?
   - Are compliance processes documented and regularly reviewed?
   - Is there proactive engagement with regulators and standard-setters?
5. **Promote Transparency and Accountability**
   - Are ESG goals measurable, time-bound, and reported with clear metrics?
   - Are there transparent mechanisms for stakeholder feedback and dialogue?
   - Does the audit committee challenge management on gaps between ESG commitments and outcomes?
6. **Embed ESG Across the Organization**
   - Is ESG governance embedded beyond the boardroom into policies and operations?
   - Are employees trained and incentivized to support ESG objectives?
   - Is cross-functional collaboration encouraged to tackle ESG challenges holistically?
7. **Leverage Technology and Data**
   - Are reliable systems in place to collect, analyze, and report ESG data?
   - Is the quality and integrity of ESG data regularly validated?
   - Does the committee understand how technology supports ESG transparency and controls?

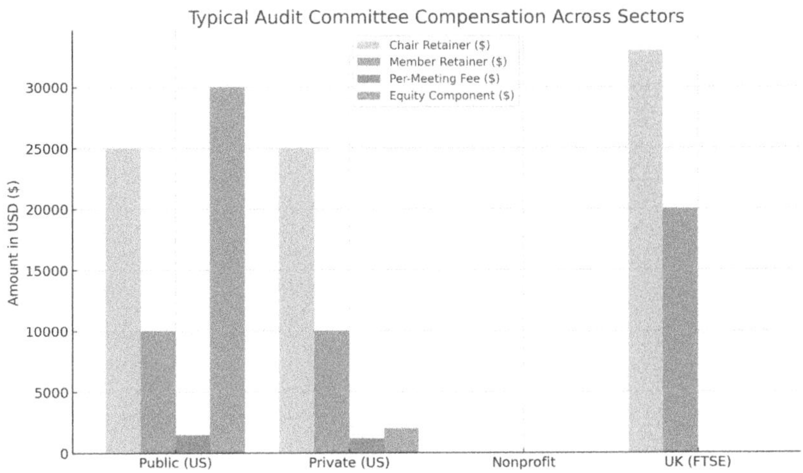

Figure A.1 Audit Committee Comp across Sectors.

8. Foster a Culture of Ethical Leadership

- Does the board model and reinforce ethical behaviors related to ESG?
- Are whistleblower and grievance mechanisms active, trusted, and responsive?
- Is there continuous dialogue on ESG ethics and its impact on reputation?

Index

D

E

F

G

H

I

L

O

P

R

S

For Product Safety Concerns and Information please contact our EU representative GPSR@taylorandfrancis.com
Taylor & Francis Verlag GmbH, Kaufingerstraße 24, 80331 München, Germany

www.ingramcontent.com/pod-product-compliance
Ingram Content Group UK Ltd.
Pitfield, Milton Keynes, MK11 3LW, UK
UKHW020205200926
475702UK00004B/617
9781041077381